Mmmm...
Salads

Mmmm...
Salads

First published in 2011

LOVE FOOD is an imprint of Parragon Books Ltd

Parragon
Queen Street House
4 Queen Street
Bath BA1 1HE, UK

ISBN: 978-1-4454-2441-5

Printed in China

Internal design by Talking Design
Introduction by Linda Doeser

Notes for the Reader
This book uses both metric and imperial measurements. Follow the same units of measurement throughout; do not mix metric and imperial. All spoon measurements are level: teaspoons are assumed to be 5 ml, and tablespoons are assumed to be 15 ml. Unless otherwise stated, milk is assumed to be full fat, eggs and individual vegetables are medium, and pepper is freshly ground black pepper.

The times given are an approximate guide only. Preparation times differ according to the techniques used by different people and the cooking times may also vary from those given. Optional ingredients, variations or serving suggestions have not been included in the calculations.

Recipes using raw or very lightly cooked eggs should be avoided by infants, the elderly, pregnant women, convalescents and anyone suffering from an illness. Pregnant and breastfeeding women are advised to avoid eating peanuts and peanut products. Sufferers from nut allergies should be aware that some of the ready-made ingredients used in the recipes in this book may contain nuts. Always check the packaging before use.

contents

introduction

It is not news that governments and nutritionists in many countries have been recommending for a long time that we eat more fruit and vegetables – sometimes five a day, sometimes seven. Nor is it news that many adults and children in the western world have been gaining too much weight and putting their health at risk. Nevertheless, it isn't always easy to ensure that the family eats healthily – life is busy so shopping and cooking may sometimes take a back seat.

Also, after-school clubs and classes can mean different mealtimes for different family members, appealing fast-food outlets offer apparently attractive and easy options and everyone has different tastes with one family member who doesn't like peas and someone else who dislikes carrots. What is news is that the recipes for salads in this book are so scrumptious and varied that five – or even seven – a day is made easy for the family cook to prepare and for everyone to eat and enjoy.

If you think of salad as simply being green salad leaves, cucumber, tomatoes and some cold meat or grated cheese, you'll be really surprised by the irresistible array of tasty dishes in the following pages. There are no hard-and-fast rules about what makes a salad. Green salad leaves remain a popular choice, but other ingredients include fruit, such as strawberries and mango; pulses, such as lentils and butter beans; and vegetables, such as asparagus and peppers. Although we tend to think of salads as made from raw ingredients, cooked grains and beans are delicious additions and some of the most alluring salads are served warm.

top tips for success

- One of the keynotes of salads is texture. Limp leaves will never become crisper with the addition of dressing, watery raw tomatoes are inedible, carrots must be crisp not bendy and avocados must be creamily ripe. Ingredients should be as fresh as possible, ideally prepared on the day of purchase. This is not just essential for taste and texture, but also for nutrition as many vitamins can be lost during storage.

- The variety of salad leaves available these days is astonishing. Apart from the familiar lettuces, such as round, Cos, Iceberg and Little Gem, there are many other varieties such as oakleaf, lollo rosso and lollo biondo. Endive, curly endive and radicchio are all members of the chicory family and share a characteristic bitter flavour that peps up milder leaves. Rocket, young spinach leaves and watercress also have a peppery taste that gives bite to mixed salads. Lamb's lettuce, also known as corn salad and mâche, is not a true lettuce and is a useful winter vegetable with a slightly nutty flavour. As well as combining sweet, mild and peppery leaves for a delicious range of flavours, use a mixture of colours for visual appeal – we eat with our eyes as well as our mouths.

- Radishes are great for pepping up salads and adding colour. There are lots of different varieties, the most popular being the small round red ones and the red and white elongated French breakfast radishes. They are available all year round and are milder in the spring. Buy them with their leaves intact as, if these are green and vigorous, it is an indication of freshness. Store them in the salad drawer of the refrigerator for up to 4 days.

- There are numerous varieties of tomatoes but not all are suited to salads. Cherry tomatoes, whether red or yellow, have a sweet flavour and appealing appearance. Children in particular like these miniatures. By contrast, beef tomatoes may be as large as 10 cm/4 inches in diameter. They are usually ridged and may be deep red or orange. They have an excellent flavour and are ideal for salads. Round tomatoes are also known as salad tomatoes. However, some varieties have been carefully bred to withstand the handling of long transportation and storage and are rather insipid. Choose vine tomatoes to ensure a richer taste and better texture. Store tomatoes in a bowl in the kitchen rather than in the refrigerator.

- Raw onions, particularly sweet, mild red, white and Spanish onions, add a delicious flavour to salads. If you are concerned about their astringency, soak them in salted water or sprinkle with salt and leave for 15 minutes, then rinse well. Either dice finely or cut into wafer-thin slices. Spring onions are a traditional ingredient in mixed salads. Both the white bulbs and the green tops may be used. Store spring onions in the salad drawer of the refrigerator and other onions in a cool, dry place.

- Cucumbers may be smooth or ridged and are available in a range of lengths. It's a matter of personal taste whether you peel them but if you don't, wash them thoroughly as they are often given a wax coating to make them shiny. You can use a canelle knife or lemon stripper to cut narrow grooves in the peel so that when the cucumber is sliced it has an attractive scalloped edge. Always slice cucumber as thinly as possible. Store in the salad drawer of the refrigerator for up to 1 week. If it has a plastic cover, remove this completely before using.

- Small waxy potatoes, often described as 'salad potatoes' in supermarkets are not only delicious with mayonnaise and chives in a classic potato salad, but are also delicious in warm salads partnered with bacon or spicy sausage. Special salad varieties include Pink Fir Apple, Finger Potatoes and La Ratte. Store them in a cool, dark, airy place.

- Avocados have to be picked before they ripen, otherwise they immediately fall off the tree. Buy them a few days before you intend to use them and leave at room temperature for 4–5 days. When ripe, the fruit will 'give' slightly when gently squeezed but will not feel soft. Do not allow the skin to develop dark patches. If you need to store the ripe avocado for a little longer, put it into the refrigerator.

- Celery is ideal for adding flavour and bulk to salads. It has a crunchy texture and distinctive flavour which is perfect for most salads. It has become a common household staple along with potatoes. Choose celery heads with leaves that look bright green and fresh. The leaves can also be used in salads or as a garnish. Store in a plastic bag or clingfilm to prevent the stalks going limp.

herb vinaigrette

makes about 150 ml/5 fl oz
- 125 ml/4 fl oz olive oil
- 3 tbsp white wine vinegar or lemon juice
- 1½ tbsp chopped fresh herbs, such as chives, parsley or mint
- 1 tsp Dijon mustard
- ½ tsp caster sugar
- salt and pepper

1 Put all the ingredients in a screw-top jar, secure the lid and shake vigorously until a thick emulsion forms. Taste and adjust the seasoning if necessary.

2 Use at once or store in an airtight container in the refrigerator for up to 3 days. Always whisk or shake the dressing before using, and strain through a fine non-metallic sieve if the herbs begin to darken.

basil, chive & lemon dressing

serves 4–6
- 1 tbsp fresh dill, chopped
- 20 chives, snipped
- 4 tbsp basil, chive and lemon vinegar
- 1 tsp Dijon mustard
- 2 tbsp olive oil
- 1 tbsp fresh lemon juice
- salt and pepper

1 Put the dill and chives in a mixing bowl and combine.

2 Whisk together the vinegar, mustard, oil and lemon juice. Season to taste with salt and pepper and pour into the mixing bowl with the dill and chives.

3 Serve immediately or store, covered, in the refrigerator and bring to room temperature before serving.

garlic, chilli & oregano oil

makes about 225 ml/8 fl oz

- 5 garlic cloves, halved lengthways
- 2 tbsp deseeded and chopped red hot chilli
- 1 tsp dried oregano
- 225 ml/8 fl oz rapessed oil

1 Preheat the oven to 150°C/300°F/ Gas Mark 2. Combine the garlic, chilli and oregano with the oil in an ovenproof glass measuring jug. Place on a glass pie plate in the centre of the oven and heat for 1½–2 hours.

2 Remove from the oven, allow to cool, then strain through muslin into a clean jar. Store, covered, in the refrigerator. You can also leave the garlic and chilli pieces in the oil and strain before using.

tomato dressing

serves 2–4

- 2 tbsp balsamic vinegar, or red or white wine vinegar
- 4–6 tbsp extra virgin olive oil
- 1 tsp Dijon mustard
- pinch of caster sugar
- 1 tbsp torn fresh basil leaves
- 1 tbsp chopped sun-dried tomatoes
- salt and pepper

1 Place all the ingredients in a screw-top jar, secure the top and shake well. Alternatively, beat all the ingredients together in a small bowl. Use as much oil as you like.

2 If you have just salad leaves to dress, 4 tablespoons of oil will be sufficient, but if you have heavier ingredients such as potatoes, you will need about 6 tablespoons of oil.

3 Use the dressing at once. If you want to store it, do not add the herbs – it will then keep for 3–4 days in the refrigerator.

Mmmm...
meat

roast beef salad

serves 4
- 750 g/1 lb 10 oz beef fillet, trimmed of any visible fat
- 2 tsp Worcestershire sauce
- 3 tbsp olive oil
- 400 g/14 oz French beans
- 100 g/3½ oz dried orecchiette
- 2 red onions, finely sliced
- 1 large head radicchio, leaves separated
- 50 g/1¾ oz green olives, stoned
- 50 g/1¾ oz shelled hazelnuts, whole
- pepper

dressing
- 1 tsp Dijon mustard
- 2 tbsp white wine vinegar
- 5 tbsp olive oil

1 Preheat the oven to 220°C/425°F/Gas Mark 7. Rub the beef with pepper to taste and Worcestershire sauce. Heat 2 tablespoons of the oil in a small roasting tin over a high heat, add the beef and sear on all sides. Transfer the dish to the preheated oven and roast for 30 minutes. Remove and leave to cool.

2 Bring a saucepan of water to the boil, add the beans and cook for 5 minutes, or until just tender. Remove with a slotted spoon, keeping the cooking water and refresh the beans under cold running water. Drain and put into a large bowl.

3 Return the bean cooking water to the boil, add the pasta and cook for 11 minutes, or until tender. Drain, return to the saucepan and toss with the remaining oil.

4 Add the pasta to the beans with the onions, radicchio leaves, olives and hazelnuts, mix gently and transfer to a serving bowl or dish. Arrange some thinly sliced beef on top.

5 To make the dressing, put all the ingredients into a small screw-top jar and shake until well blended. Pour over the salad and serve immediately with extra sliced beef. Season with extra pepper, if liked.

warm beef salad niçoise

serves 4

- 4 fillet steaks, about 115 g/4 oz each, trimmed of any visible fat
- 2 tbsp red wine vinegar
- 2 tbsp orange juice
- 2 tsp English mustard
- 2 eggs
- 175 g/6 oz new potatoes
- 115 g/4 oz French beans, trimmed
- 175 g/6 oz mixed salad leaves, such as baby spinach, rocket and mizuna
- 1 yellow pepper, peeled, skinned and cut into strips
- 175 g/6 oz cherry tomatoes, halved
- black olives, stoned (optional)
- 2 tsp extra virgin olive oil

1 Place the steaks in a shallow dish. Blend the vinegar with 1 tablespoon of orange juice and 1 teaspoon of mustard. Pour over the steaks, cover and leave in the refrigerator for at least 30 minutes. Turn over halfway through the marinating time. Place the eggs in a pan and cover with cold water. Bring to the boil, then reduce the heat to a simmer and cook for 10 minutes. Remove and plunge the eggs into cold water. Once cold, shell and reserve. Meanwhile, place the potatoes in a saucepan and cover with cold water. Bring to the boil, cover and simmer for 15 minutes, or until tender when pierced with a fork. Drain and reserve.

2 Bring a saucepan of water to the boil, add the beans and cook for 5 minutes, or until just tender. Drain, plunge into cold water and drain again. Arrange the potatoes and beans on top of the salad leaves together with the yellow pepper, cherry tomatoes and olives, if using. Blend the remaining orange juice and mustard with the olive oil and reserve. Heat a griddle pan until smoking. Drain the steaks and cook for 3–5 minutes on each side or according to personal preference. Slice the steaks and arrange on top of the salad, then pour over the dressing and serve.

beef satay salad

serves 4
- 2 sirloin steaks, about 225 g/8 oz each, trimmed of any visible fat
- 2 tbsp soy sauce
- 1 tbsp lime juice
- 1 garlic clove, crushed
- 1 tsp dried chilli flakes
- 350 g/12 oz Chinese leaves, shredded
- ¼ cucumber, thinly sliced
- 4 spring onions, sliced
- fresh coriander leaves and sliced red chilli pepper, to garnish
- lime wedges, to serve

satay dressing
- 2 tbsp crunchy peanut butter
- 3 tbsp coconut milk
- 1 tbsp soy sauce
- 1 tbsp lime juice
- 2 tsp soft brown sugar

1 Place the steaks in a shallow dish. Mix together the soy sauce, lime juice, garlic and chilli flakes and pour over the steaks. Cover and leave to marinate at room temperature for 1 hour.

2 Heat a cast-iron griddle pan until very hot. Add the steaks and cook for 3–5 minutes on each side, depending on how well done you like your steak. Transfer the steaks to a plate and cover and leave to rest for 5 minutes.

3 To make the satay dressing, place all the ingredients in a small saucepan and heat gently, stirring all the time, until the peanut butter has melted. Simmer for 1 minute. If the dressing becomes too thick add a little water and stir well to make a pouring consistency.

4 Mix together the Chinese leaves, cucumber and spring onions and place on a serving platter. Thinly slice the steaks and arrange on top of the salad. Drizzle over the satay dressing and garnish with coriander leaves and chilli pepper. Serve with lime wedges.

steak waldorf salad

serves 4

- 2 fillet steaks, about 175 g/6 oz each and 2.5 cm/1 inch thick
- olive oil or sunflower oil, for brushing
- 1 tbsp wholegrain mustard
- 150 ml/5 fl oz mayonnaise
- 1 tbsp lemon juice
- 500 g/1 lb 2 oz eating apples
- 4 celery sticks, thinly sliced
- 70 g/2½ oz walnut halves, broken into pieces
- 100 g/3½ oz mixed salad leaves
- pepper
- fresh wholemeal bread, to serve

1 Heat a cast-iron griddle pan or heavy-based frying pan over a medium heat. Brush each steak with oil and season to taste with pepper. Add the steaks to the pan and cook for 6–7 minutes for rare or 8–10 minutes for medium, turning the steaks frequently and brushing once or twice with oil. Remove from the pan and reserve.

2 Meanwhile, stir the mustard into the mayonnaise. Put the lemon juice into a large bowl. Peel and core the apples, then cut them into small chunks and immediately toss them in the lemon juice. Stir in the mustard mayonnaise. Add the celery and walnuts to the apple mixture and toss together.

3 Arrange the salad leaves on 4 plates, then divide the apple mixture between them. Slice the steaks, arrange on top of the salad and serve immediately with bread.

rare beef pasta salad

serves 4

- 450 g/1 lb rump or sirloin steak in 1 piece
- 450 g/1 lb dried fusilli
- 4 tbsp olive oil
- 2 tbsp lime juice
- 2 tbsp Thai fish sauce
- 2 tsp clear honey
- 4 spring onions, sliced
- 1 cucumber, peeled and cut into 2.5-cm/1-inch chunks
- 3 tomatoes, cut into wedges
- 3 tsp finely chopped fresh mint
- salt and pepper

1 Season the steak to taste with salt and pepper, then grill or pan-fry for 4 minutes on each side. Leave to rest for 5 minutes, then, using a sharp knife, slice the steak thinly across the grain and reserve until required.

2 Meanwhile, bring a large pan of lightly salted water to the boil over a medium heat. Add the pasta and cook for 8–10 minutes, until tender but still firm to the bite. Drain thoroughly, refresh in cold water and drain again. Toss the pasta in the oil.

3 Mix the lime juice, fish sauce and honey together in a small pan and cook over a medium heat for about 2 minutes.

4 Add the spring onions, cucumber, tomato wedges and mint to the pan, then add the steak and mix well. Season with salt to taste.

5 Transfer the pasta to a large warmed serving dish and top with the steak mixture. Serve just warm or leave to cool completely.

beef salad with noodles

serves 4
- 350 g/12 oz sirloin steak, trimmed of any visible fat
- 90 g/3¼ oz egg noodles
- 1 small red onion, halved and thinly sliced into crescents
- 6 radishes, sliced
- 4 good handfuls of peppery leaves such as tatsoi, mustard greens and rocket
- 1½ tbsp groundnut oil
- 1 tsp Szechuan pepper, crushed

marinade
- 4 tsp Chinese rice wine or dry sherry
- ½ tbsp soy sauce
- 4 tsp sugar
- 2 tbsp hoisin sauce
- 2.5-cm/1-inch piece fresh ginger, squeezed in a garlic press

dressing
- 2 tsp Szechuan pepper, crushed
- 1½ tbsp light soy sauce
- 1½ tbsp rice vinegar
- 2 tbsp cold-pressed sesame oil

1 Slice the beef into neat strips measuring about 1 x 4 cm/½ x 1½ inches. Combine the marinade ingredients and pour over the beef. Leave at room temperature for 30 minutes or in the refrigerator for up to 2 days.

2 Cook the noodles in a saucepan of boiling water for 4 minutes, or according to the instructions on the packet, until soft. Allow to cool. Snip into shorter lengths. Whisk the dressing ingredients until well blended. Combine the noodles, onion, radishes and salad leaves in a large bowl. Whisk the dressing again and pour two thirds of it over the salad. Toss to distribute the noodles, then divide between individual serving plates.

3 Heat a wok over a medium–high heat, then add the groundnut oil and the Szechuan pepper. Stir for a few seconds to flavour the oil. Add the beef and marinade, and stir-fry for 4–5 minutes until caramelized. Remove with a slotted spoon, and scatter over the salad. Pour over the remaining dressing.

hot & sour beef salad

serves 4
- 1 tsp black peppercorns
- 1 tsp coriander seeds
- 1 dried red bird's eye chilli
- ¼ tsp Chinese five-spice powder
- 250 g/9 oz beef fillet
- 1 tbsp dark soy sauce
- 6 spring onions
- 1 carrot
- ¼ cucumber
- 8 radishes
- 1 red onion
- ¼ head Chinese leaves
- 2 tbsp groundnut oil
- 1 garlic clove, crushed
- 1 tsp finely chopped lemon grass
- 1 tbsp chopped fresh mint
- 1 tbsp chopped fresh coriander

dressing
- 3 tbsp lime juice
- 1 tbsp light soy sauce
- 2 tsp soft light brown sugar
- 1 tsp sesame oil

1 Crush the peppercorns, coriander seeds and chilli in a mortar with a pestle, then mix with the five-spice powder and sprinkle on a plate. Brush the beef all over with soy sauce, then roll it in the spices to coat evenly.

2 Cut the spring onions into 6 cm/2½ inch lengths, then shred finely lengthways. Place in iced water until curled. Drain well.

3 Trim the carrot and cut into very thin diagonal slices. Halve the cucumber, scoop out and discard the seeds, then slice the flesh thinly. Trim the radishes and cut into flower shapes.

4 Thinly slice the onion and roughly shred the Chinese leaves. Toss all the vegetables together in a large salad bowl.

5 Heat the oil in a frying pan and fry the garlic and lemon grass until golden. Add the beef and cook for 3–4 minutes, turning once. Remove from the heat.

6 Slice the beef thinly and toss into the salad with the mint and coriander. Mix together the dressing ingredients and stir into the pan, then spoon over the salad. Serve immediately.

grilled lamb salad

serves 4
- 2 tbsp sunflower oil, plus extra for grilling
- 1 tbsp tomato purée
- ½ tbsp ground cumin
- 1 tsp lemon juice
- 1 garlic clove, crushed
- pinch of cayenne pepper
- 500 g/1 lb 2 oz lamb neck fillets, trimmed of any visible fat
- oil, for brushing
- salt and pepper
- toasted sesame seeds and sprigs of fresh flat-leaf parsley, to garnish

dressing
- 2 tbsp fresh lemon juice
- 1 tsp clear honey
- 85 g/3 oz Greek yogurt
- 2 tbsp finely shredded fresh mint
- 2 tbsp chopped fresh flat-leaf parsley
- 1 tbsp finely snipped fresh chives
- salt and pepper

1 Mix together the oil, tomato purée, cumin, lemon juice, garlic, cayenne and salt and pepper to taste in a non-metallic bowl. Add the lamb fillets and rub all over with the marinade. Cover the bowl and marinate in the fridge for at least 2 hours, but ideally overnight.

2 To make the dressing, whisk the lemon juice and honey together until the honey dissolves. Whisk in the yogurt until well blended. Stir in the herbs and add salt and pepper to taste. Cover and chill until required. Preheat the grill to high.

3 Remove the lamb from the fridge 15 minutes before you are ready to cook. Brush the grill rack with oil. Grill the lamb fillets, turning it once, for 10 minutes for medium and 12 minutes for well done. Leave the lamb to cool completely, then cover and chill until required.

4 Thinly slice the lamb fillets, then divide between 4 plates. Pour the dressing over the lamb slices, sprinkle with toasted sesame seeds and parsley and serve.

lamb kofte & herb salad

serves 4

- 400 g/14 oz lean minced lamb
- 1 small onion, finely chopped
- 2 tsp each ground coriander, ground cumin and paprika
- 1 tbsp chopped fresh coriander
- 2 tbsp chopped fresh mint
- 3 tbsp olive oil
- 6 tbsp natural yogurt
- 85 g/3 oz cucumber, grated
- 2 tsp mint sauce
- 115 g/4 oz mixed baby leaf and herb salad
- 1 tbsp lemon juice
- salt and pepper

1 Place 8 wooden skewers in a shallow bowl of cold water and leave to soak for 30 minutes. Place the lamb, onion, spices and coriander and mint in a food processor with plenty of salt and pepper. Process for 1–2 minutes until finely minced. Transfer to a bowl and cover and chill in the refrigerator for 30 minutes. Preheat the grill to medium–high.

2 Divide the mixture into 8. Wrap the mixture around the soaked wooden skewers to form oval shapes. Brush with a little of the oil and grill for 15–20 minutes, turning frequently until cooked through.

3 Meanwhile, mix the yogurt, cucumber and mint sauce together in a small bowl and season with salt and pepper.

4 Place the salad leaves in a large bowl. Whisk together the rest of the oil with the lemon juice and season to taste. Pour the dressing over the salad leaves and toss to coat. Serve the hot koftes, on or off the skewers, with the salad and cucumber and mint yogurt.

roast pork & pumpkin salad

serves 4–6

- 1 small pumpkin, about 1.6 kg/3 lb 8 oz, cut in half and deseeded
- 2 red onions, cut into wedges
- olive oil, for brushing
- 100 g/3½ oz French beans, topped and tailed and cut in half
- 600 g/1 lb 5 oz roast pork, trimmed of any visible fat and cut into bite-sized chunks
- large handful of rocket leaves
- 100 g/3½ oz feta cheese, drained and crumbled
- 2 tbsp pine kernels, toasted
- 2 tbsp chopped fresh flat-leaf parsley

dressing

- 6 tbsp extra virgin olive oil
- 3 tbsp balsamic vinegar
- ½ tsp sugar
- ½ tsp Dijon or wholegrain mustard

1 Preheat the oven to 200°C/400°F/Gas Mark 6. Cut the pumpkin halves into wedges about 4 cm/1½ inches wide. Very lightly brush the pumpkin and onion wedges with the olive oil, place in a roasting pan and roast for 25–30 minutes until the pumpkin and onions are tender but holding their shape.

2 Bring a saucepan of water to the boil, add the beans and cook for 5 minutes, or until just tender. Remove with a slotted spoon and refresh the beans under cold running water. Drain and put into a large bowl.

3 Remove the pumpkin and onion wedges from the oven as soon as they are tender-crisp and leave to cool completely. When the pumpkin is cool, peel and cut into bite-sized pieces.

4 To make the dressing, put all the ingredients into a small screw-top jar and shake until well blended.

5 Put the pumpkin wedges, onions, beans, pork, rocket, feta, pine kernels and parsley in a large bowl, pour over the dressing and gently toss until coated. Divide between individual bowls and serve.

hoisin pork with ribbon salad

serves 4
- 450 g/1 lb pork fillet
- 3 tbsp hoisin sauce
- 175 g/6 oz carrots
- ½ cucumber
- 4 spring onions, finely shredded
- 4 radishes, very thinly sliced
- 2 tbsp sesame seeds

dressing
- 2 tbsp toasted sesame oil
- 2 tbsp rice vinegar

1 Slice the pork fillet into 2 pieces and place in a shallow dish. Pour over the hoisin sauce, cover and leave to marinate at room temperature for 1 hour.

2 Preheat the oven to 190°C/375°F/ Gas Mark 5. Place the pork fillet on a wire rack set over a roasting tin half filled with water (this helps to keep the pork moist during cooking). Roast for 35–40 minutes until the pork is cooked through and lightly charred in places. Cool for 10 minutes.

3 Use a potato peeler to peel the carrots and cucumber into thin ribbons. Place in a bowl and toss together with the spring onions and radishes.

4 Heat a non-stick frying pan and add the sesame seeds. Cook over a medium heat for 3–4 minutes until lightly toasted. Add to the salad. To make the dressing, put the sesame oil and vinegar into a small screw-top jar and shake until well blended. Pour half over the salad and toss well to mix.

5 Slice the pork fillet and arrange on individual serving plates with the ribbon salad on the side. Drizzle the rest of the dressing over the pork and serve immediately.

pork & cucumber salad

serves 4

- 450 g / 1 lb pork fillet, trimmed of any visible fat
- 6 spring onions, halved lengthways and sliced into 3
- 1 ridge cucumber
- 4 handfuls shredded crisp lettuce
- 20 g / ¾ oz fresh coriander leaves
- 10 g / ¼ oz fresh mint leaves
- 4 tbsp dry-roasted peanuts, lightly crushed
- finely grated zest of 1 lime
- 1 tsp salt
- 1 tsp sugar
- 2 tsp sesame oil
- 1 tbsp groundnut oil

marinade

- 2 small red chillies, deseeded and very finely chopped
- 4 tbsp sugar
- 3 tbsp Thai fish sauce
- 4 tbsp lime juice
- 4 tbsp rice vinegar

1 Thinly slice the pork diagonally. Cut each slice in half lengthways. Put in a bowl with the spring onions. Peel the cucumber, halve lengthways and scoop out the seeds. Thinly slice diagonally and put in a bowl.

2 To make the marinade, use a large mortar and pestle and pound the chopped chillies and the sugar to a watery red paste. Add the fish sauce, lime juice and rice vinegar, stirring to dissolve the sugar. Pour into a measuring jug. Pour one half over the pork and onions, and one half over the cucumber. Leave to marinate for 1 hour, then drain, reserving the cucumber marinade.

3 Put the shredded lettuce, coriander and mint in a bowl, and toss to mix. Divide between individual serving plates. Arrange the cucumber slices on top and dress with the reserved marinade.

4 Mix the nuts with the lime zest, salt and sugar. Heat a wok over a high heat, then add the oils. Stir-fry the pork for 5 minutes until cooked through and slightly caramelized. Arrange the pork slices on top of the cucumber and sprinkle with the nut mixture. Serve immediately.

hot sausage & potato salad

serves 4
- 700 g/1 lb 9 oz new potatoes, halved
- 1 tbsp sunflower oil
- 6 thick pork sausages
- 2 onions, sliced into thin wedges
- chopped fresh flat-leaf parsley, to garnish (optional)

dressing
- 4 tbsp olive oil
- 1 tbsp white wine vinegar
- 2 tsp wholegrain mustard
- 2 tsp clear honey
- salt and pepper

1 Place the potatoes in a saucepan and cover with cold water. Bring to the boil, cover and simmer for 15 minutes, or until tender when pierced with a fork.

2 Meanwhile, heat the sunflower oil in a large frying pan and fry the sausages for 5 minutes. Add the onions to the pan and continue cooking for a further 8–10 minutes, turning frequently, until the sausages are cooked through and the onions are golden and tender. Remove the onions and sausages from the pan and drain on kitchen paper. Slice each sausage diagonally into 4 pieces.

3 Drain the potatoes and place in a large bowl with the onions and sausages.

4 To make the dressing, put all the ingredients in a small screw-top jar and shake until well blended. Pour over the hot salad and toss well to coat. Serve immediately, garnished with chopped parsley, if using.

spicy sausage pasta salad

serves 4

- 125 g/4½ oz dried conchiglie
- 2 tbsp olive oil
- 1 medium onion, chopped
- 2 garlic cloves, crushed
- 1 small yellow pepper, deseeded and cut into matchsticks
- 175 g/6 oz spicy pork sausage, such as chorizo, Italian pepperoni or salami, skinned and sliced
- 2 tbsp red wine
- 1 tbsp red wine vinegar
- 125 g/4½ oz mixed salad leaves
- salt

1 Bring a large saucepan of lightly salted water to the boil. Add the pasta and return to the boil. Cook for 10–12 minutes until just tender. Drain the pasta and reserve.

2 Heat the oil in a pan over a medium heat. Add the onion and fry until translucent. Stir in the garlic, yellow pepper and sliced sausage and cook for about 3–4 minutes, stirring once or twice.

3 Add the wine, vinegar and reserved pasta to the pan, stir to blend well and bring the mixture just to the boil over a medium heat.

4 Arrange the salad leaves on 4 large serving plates, spoon over the warm sausage and pasta mixture and serve immediately.

artichoke & chorizo salad

serves 8

- 12 small globe artichokes
- juice of ½ lemon
- 2 tbsp olive oil
- 1 small orange-fleshed melon, such as cantaloupe
- 200 g/7 oz chorizo sausage, outer casing removed
- fresh tarragon or flat-leaf parsley sprigs, to garnish

dressing

- 3 tbsp extra virgin olive oil
- 1 tbsp red wine vinegar
- 1 tsp prepared mustard
- 1 tbsp chopped fresh tarragon
- salt and pepper

1 Cut the artichokes into quarters and brush with lemon juice to prevent discoloration.

2 Heat the olive oil in a large, heavy-based frying pan. Add the prepared artichokes and fry, stirring frequently, for 5 minutes, or until the artichoke leaves are golden brown. Remove from the frying pan, transfer to a large serving bowl and leave to cool.

3 To prepare the melon, cut in half and scoop out the seeds with a spoon. Cut the flesh into bite-sized cubes. Add to the cooled artichokes. Cut the chorizo into bite-sized chunks and add to the melon and artichokes.

4 To make the dressing, put all the ingredients into a small screw-top jar and shake until well blended. Just before serving, pour the dressing over the prepared salad ingredients and toss together. Serve the salad garnished with tarragon.

onion & herb salad with chorizo

serves 2

- 1 tbsp sunflower oil
- 1 small onion, finely sliced
- 250 g/9 oz canned butter beans, drained and rinsed
- 1 tsp balsamic vinegar
- 2 chorizo sausages, sliced diagonally
- 1 small tomato, diced
- 2 tbsp harissa paste
- 85 g/3 oz mixed herb salad

1 Heat the oil in a non-stick frying pan over a medium heat, add the onion and cook, stirring frequently, until softened but not browned. Add the beans and cook for a further minute, then add the vinegar, stirring well. Keep warm.

2 Meanwhile, heat a separate dry frying pan over a medium heat, add the chorizo slices and cook, turning occasionally, until lightly browned. Remove with a slotted spoon and drain on kitchen paper.

3 Mix the tomato and harissa paste together in a small bowl. Divide the herb salad between 2 plates, spoon over the bean mixture and scatter over the warm chorizo slices. Top with a spoonful of the tomato and harissa mixture and serve immediately.

warm bacon & egg salad

serves 4

- 2 cos lettuce hearts, roughly torn
- 4 eggs
- 2 tbsp sunflower oil
- 2 thick slices of white bread, crusts removed, cut into cubes
- 225 g/8 oz smoked bacon lardons
- 12 cherry tomatoes, halved

dressing

- 2 tbsp extra virgin olive oil
- 1 tbsp red wine vinegar
- 1 tsp Dijon mustard
- pepper

1 To make the dressing, put all the ingredients into a small screw-top jar and shake until well blended. Put the lettuce leaves in a salad bowl.

2 Place the eggs in a saucepan and cover with cold water. Bring to the boil and boil for 4 minutes. Drain and plunge the eggs into cold water for 2 minutes. Peel off the shells and cut into quarters.

3 Heat the sunflower oil in a large frying pan and fry the bread cubes for 3–4 minutes, turning frequently until golden brown. Remove with a slotted spoon and set aside.

4 Add the bacon lardons to the pan and fry over a medium–high heat until crisp and golden. Add the tomatoes and dressing to the pan and cook for a further minute.

5 Gently toss the bacon, tomatoes and dressing into the salad leaves. Add the quartered eggs and scatter over the croûtons. Serve immediately.

bacon, lettuce & tomato salad

serves 4

- 8 thick rashers back bacon
- 1 iceberg lettuce, cut into 12 wedges
- 2 beef tomatoes, sliced into wedges
- ¼ cucumber, thickly sliced
- ½ ripe avocado, sliced
- 1 tbsp lemon juice
- 85 g/3 oz Cheddar cheese, roughly grated (optional)

dressing

- 4 tbsp mayonnaise
- 2 tbsp soured cream
- 1 tbsp milk
- 2 tsp wholegrain mustard
- salt and pepper

1 Preheat the grill to high. Place the bacon rashers on the grill pan and grill for 3–4 minutes, turning once, until crisp.

2 To make the dressing, place the mayonnaise, soured cream, milk and mustard in a bowl and whisk together until smooth. Season with salt and pepper.

3 Divide the lettuce wedges between 4 serving plates with the tomatoes and cucumber. Toss the avocado slices in the lemon juice and add to the salads.

4 Drizzle the dressing over the salads. Halve the bacon rashers and stack on top of the salads. Sprinkle over the grated cheese, if using. Serve immediately.

spinach & bacon salad

serves 4
- 4 tbsp olive oil
- 4 rashers of streaky bacon, diced
- 1 thick slice of white bread, crusts removed, cut into cubes
- 450 g/1 lb fresh spinach, torn or shredded

1 Heat 2 tablespoons of the olive oil over a high heat in a large frying pan. Add the diced bacon to the pan and cook for 3–4 minutes, or until crisp. Remove with a slotted spoon, draining carefully, and set aside.

2 Toss the cubes of bread in the fat remaining in the pan over a high heat for about 4 minutes, or until crisp and golden. Remove the croûtons with a slotted spoon, draining carefully, and set them aside.

3 Add the remaining oil to the frying pan and heat. Toss the spinach in the oil over a high heat for about 3 minutes, or until it has just wilted. Turn into a serving bowl and sprinkle with the bacon and croûtons. Serve immediately.

walnut, pear & crispy bacon salad

serves 4
- 4 lean bacon rashers
- 85 g/3 oz walnut halves
- 2 Red William pears, cored and sliced lengthways
- 1 tbsp lemon juice
- 175 g/6 oz watercress, tough stalks removed

dressing
- 3 tbsp extra virgin olive oil
- 2 tbsp lemon juice
- ½ tsp clear honey
- salt and pepper

1 Preheat the grill to high. Place the bacon rashers on the grill pan and grill for 3–4 minutes, turning once, until crisp. Set aside to cool, then cut into 1-cm/½-inch pieces.

2 Meanwhile, heat a dry frying pan over a medium heat and lightly toast the walnuts, shaking the pan frequently, for 3 minutes, or until lightly browned. Set aside to cool.

3 Toss the pear slices in the lemon juice to prevent discoloration. Put the watercress, walnuts, pears and bacon into a salad bowl.

4 To make the dressing, place the oil, lemon juice and honey in a bowl and whisk together until smooth. Season to taste with salt and pepper, then pour over the salad. Toss well to combine and serve.

artichoke & prosciutto salad

serves 4

- 275 g/9¾ oz canned artichoke hearts in oil, drained
- 4 small tomatoes
- 25 g/1 oz sun-dried tomatoes in oil, drained
- 40 g/1½ oz prosciutto
- 25 g/1 oz black olives, stoned and halved
- handful of fresh basil sprigs
- fresh crusty bread, to serve

dressing

- 3 tbsp olive oil
- 1 tbsp white wine vinegar
- 1 garlic clove, crushed
- ½ tsp mild mustard
- 1 tsp clear honey
- salt and pepper

1 Make sure the artichoke hearts are thoroughly drained, then cut them into quarters and put into a serving bowl. Cut each fresh tomato into wedges. Slice the sun-dried tomatoes into thin strips. Cut the prosciutto into thin strips and add to the bowl with the tomatoes and olive halves.

2 Keeping a few basil sprigs whole for garnishing, tear the remainder of the leaves into small pieces and add to the bowl containing the other salad ingredients.

3 To make the dressing, put all the ingredients into a small screw-top jar and shake until well blended.

4 Pour the dressing over the salad and toss together. Garnish the salad with a few basil sprigs and serve with crusty bread.

prosciutto with melon & asparagus

serves 4

- 225 g/8 oz asparagus spears
- 1 small or ½ medium-sized Galia or cantaloupe melon
- 55 g/2 oz prosciutto, thinly sliced
- 150 g/5½ oz mixed salad leaves, such as herb salad with rocket
- 85 g/3 oz fresh raspberries
- 1 tbsp freshly shaved Parmesan cheese
- salt

dressing

- 1 tbsp balsamic vinegar
- 2 tbsp raspberry vinegar
- 2 tbsp orange juice

1 Trim the asparagus, cutting in half if very long. Cook in lightly salted, boiling water over a medium heat for 5 minutes, or until tender. Drain and plunge into cold water then drain again and reserve.

2 Cut the melon in half and scoop out the seeds. Cut into small wedges and cut away the rind. Separate the prosciutto slices, cut in half and wrap around the melon wedges.

3 Arrange the salad leaves on a large serving platter and place the melon wedges on top together with the asparagus spears.

4 Scatter over the raspberries and Parmesan cheese shavings. To make the dressing, put all the ingredients into a small screw-top jar and shake until well blended. Pour over the salad and serve.

spinach & pancetta salad

serves 4

- 275 g/9¾ oz baby spinach leaves
- 2 tbsp olive oil
- 150 g/5½ oz pancetta
- 280 g/10 oz mixed wild mushrooms, sliced

dressing

- 5 tbsp olive oil
- 1 tbsp balsamic vinegar
- 1 tsp Dijon mustard
- pinch of sugar
- salt and pepper

1 To make the dressing, put all the ingredients into a small screw-top jar and shake until well blended. Rinse the baby spinach under cold running water, then drain and place in a large salad bowl.

2 Heat the oil in a large frying pan. Add the pancetta and fry for 3 minutes. Add the mushrooms and cook for 3–4 minutes, or until tender.

3 Pour the dressing into the frying pan and immediately turn the fried mixture and dressing into the bowl with the spinach. Toss until coated with the dressing and serve immediately.

pastrami & pepper antipasti salad

serves 4

- 1 iceberg lettuce
- 1 x 285 g/10 oz jar chargrilled pepper antipasti in oil
- 115 g/4 oz sunblush tomatoes in oil
- 115 g/4 oz green olives, stoned
- 115 g/4 oz wafer thin pastrami
- fresh basil leaves, to garnish

dressing

- 2 tbsp balsamic vinegar
- 1 tsp Dijon mustard
- pinch of sugar
- salt and pepper

1 Tear the lettuce into small chunks and place in a serving bowl. Drain the pepper antipasti and sunblush tomatoes reserving 4 tablespoons of the oil. Roughly chop the peppers and tomatoes and toss into the lettuce with the olives.

2 To make the dressing, put the reserved oil and the rest of the dressing ingredients into a small screw-top jar and shake until well blended. Pour half the dressing over the salad and toss well to mix. Arrange the pastrami in ruffles on top of the salad. Serve drizzled with the rest of the dressing and garnished with basil leaves.

prosciutto & salami salad with figs

serves 6
- 6 ripe figs
- 6 thin slices prosciutto
- 12 thin slices salami
- 1 small bunch of fresh basil, separated into small sprigs
- a few fresh mint sprigs
- handful of rocket leaves

dressing
- 2 tbsp lemon juice
- 4 tbsp extra virgin olive oil
- salt and pepper

1 Trim the stems of the figs to leave just a short length, then cut the figs into quarters. Arrange the prosciutto and salami on a large serving platter.

2 Wash and dry the herbs and rocket and put in a bowl with the prepared figs. To make the dressing, whisk the lemon juice and oil together in a small bowl and season well with salt and pepper.

3 Pour the dressing into the bowl with the herbs, rocket and figs. Toss carefully until all the ingredients are well coated in the dressing. Spoon the figs and salad on top of the meat on the serving platter. Serve immediately.

salami pasta salad

serves 4–6

- 350 g/12 oz dried penne
- 2 tbsp pesto sauce
- 3 tbsp olive oil
- 1 orange pepper, deseeded and diced
- 1 yellow pepper, deseeded and diced
- 1 red onion, finely diced
- 85 g/3 oz black olives, stoned
- 115 g/4 oz cherry tomatoes, halved
- 175 g/6 oz Milano salami, cut into small chunks
- 125 g/4½ oz mozzarella cheese, drained and torn into small pieces
- salt and pepper
- fresh basil sprigs, to garnish

1 Bring a large saucepan of lightly salted water to the boil. Add the pasta and return to the boil. Cook for 10–12 minutes until just tender.

2 Drain the pasta well and transfer to a bowl. Mix together the pesto sauce and olive oil and stir into the hot pasta. Leave to cool, stirring occasionally.

3 Add the peppers, onion, olives, tomatoes, salami and mozzarella cheese to the pasta and toss well to mix. Season to taste with salt and pepper. Serve garnished with the basil sprigs.

goat's cheese salad with serrano ham

serves 4
- 4 just ripe peaches, halved, stoned and cut into 6 slices
- 1 tbsp olive oil
- 2 tsp lemon juice
- 55 g/2 oz lamb's lettuce
- 55 g/2 oz curly endive
- 125 g/4½ oz mild goat's cheese, crumbled
- 4 slices Serrano ham
- 1 tbsp toasted hazelnuts, chopped
- salt and pepper

dressing
- 4 tbsp olive oil
- 2 tbsp hazelnut oil
- 2 tbsp red wine vinegar
- ½ tsp sugar
- salt and pepper

1 To make the dressing, place all the ingredients in a small bowl and whisk together well.

2 Place the peach slices in a bowl and add the olive oil and lemon juice. Turn to coat and season lightly with salt and pepper.

3 Heat a cast iron griddle pan and add the peach slices. Cook over a medium heat for 2–3 minutes, turning once, until lightly charred and just starting to soften.

4 Mix the lamb's lettuce and curly endive together in a bowl and add half the dressing. Toss well to coat and divide between 4 serving plates. Top with the warm peach slices and crumbled goat's cheese. Place a ruffled slice of ham on the top of each salad.

5 Drizzle over the rest of the dressing and scatter over the toasted hazelnuts. Serve immediately.

Mmmm...
poultry

waldorf chicken salad

serves 4
- 500 g/1 lb 2 oz red apples, diced
- 3 tbsp fresh lemon juice
- 150 ml/5 fl oz mayonnaise
- 1 head celery
- 4 shallots, sliced
- 1 garlic clove, crushed
- 90 g/3¼ oz walnuts, chopped
- 500 g/1 lb 2 oz lean cooked chicken, cubed
- 1 cos lettuce
- pepper
- chopped walnuts, to garnish

1 Place the apples in a bowl with the lemon juice and 1 tablespoon of the mayonnaise. Leave for 40 minutes or until required.

2 Slice the celery very thinly. Add the celery with the shallots, garlic and walnuts to the apple, mix and then add the remaining mayonnaise and blend thoroughly.

3 Add the chicken and mix with the other ingredients.

4 Line a serving dish with the lettuce. Pile the chicken salad into a serving bowl, sprinkle with pepper and garnish with the chopped walnuts. Serve immediately.

creamy chicken salad

serves 4

- 1 tbsp sunflower oil
- 1 tbsp cashew nuts
- 1 tbsp whole blanched almonds
- 1 onion, chopped
- 1 tbsp mild curry paste
- 4 tbsp mayonnaise
- 4 tbsp natural yogurt
- 1 tbsp mango chutney
- 450 g/1 lb boneless cooked chicken, torn into large strips
- 140 g/5 oz watercress, spinach and rocket salad
- 1 small mango, peeled, stoned and sliced
- salt and pepper
- fresh coriander leaves, to garnish

1 Heat the oil in a frying pan. Add the cashew nuts and almonds and fry for 2–3 minutes until golden. Remove with a slotted spoon and drain on kitchen paper.

2 Add the onion to the pan and fry gently for 6–7 minutes until soft and golden. Stir in the curry paste and cook for a further minute. Transfer to a bowl and cool.

3 Stir the mayonnaise, yogurt and mango chutney into the onion and mix well. Add the chicken strips to the dressing. Toss well to coat. Season with salt and pepper.

4 Place the salad leaves in a shallow serving bowl. Add the curried chicken and mango slices to the bowl and toss gently into the salad leaves. Scatter over the fried nuts and serve garnished with the coriander leaves.

braised chicken salad

serves 4

- 3 tbsp olive oil
- 1 chicken, weighing about 1.3 kg/3 lb
- 200 ml/7 fl oz dry white wine
- 1 onion, chopped
- 1 carrot, chopped
- 1 celery stalk, chopped
- 1 fresh bay leaf
- salt and pepper

marinade

- 1 tsp black peppercorns
- 4 fresh bay leaves
- 125 ml/4 fl oz olive oil
- salt

- **salad**
- 150 g/5½ oz baby spinach leaves, chopped
- 5 tender celery stalks
- 1 head chicory
- 1 tsp wine vinegar
- 1 tsp balsamic vinegar
- salt

1 Preheat the oven to 180°C/350°F/Gas Mark 4. Heat the olive oil in an ovenproof casserole over medium–high heat. Add the chicken and fry for 15 minutes, turning, until golden all over. Pour in the wine and simmer for 2 minutes, then add the remaining main ingredients. Cover tightly and transfer to the oven. Bake for 45–50 minutes, turning every 20 minutes, until the juices from the thickest part of the thigh run clear when pierced with a skewer. Discard the liquid and solids. When cool, remove and discard the skin. Strip the meat from the bone, slicing any large chunks into bite-sized pieces.

2 Arrange the chicken in a dish. Sprinkle with salt, a few peppercorns and the bay leaves. Pour in enough oil to generously coat. Cover tightly with clingfilm and marinate in the refrigerator for 1–2 days. Remove the chicken from the fridge 2 hours before serving. Place in a colander set over a bowl to drain, and leave to stand until the oil has liquefied.

3 To make the salad, combine the spinach, celery and chicory in a large serving dish. Toss with salt, enough oil from the chicken to just coat the leaves, and the wine vinegar. Arrange the chicken on top, discarding the peppercorns and bay leaves. Sprinkle with the balsamic vinegar before serving.

smoked chicken salad

serves 4–6

- 2 large, juicy beef tomatoes, sliced
- 600 g/1 lb 5 oz smoked chicken, skinned and cut into slices
- 250 g/9 oz watercress, any thick stems or yellow leaves removed, then rinsed and patted dry
- 85 g/3 oz beansprouts, soaked for 20 minutes in cold water, then drained well and patted dry
- leaves from several sprigs fresh flat-leaf parsley or coriander

dressing

- 1 ripe, soft avocado
- 2 tbsp lemon juice
- 1 tbsp tarragon vinegar
- 85 g/3 oz Greek yogurt
- 1 small garlic clove, crushed
- 1 tbsp chopped fresh tarragon leaves
- salt and pepper

1 To make the dressing, put the avocado, lemon juice and vinegar in a food processor or blender and process until smooth, scraping down the side with a rubber spatula. Add the yogurt, garlic and tarragon leaves and process again. Season with salt and pepper to taste, then transfer to a bowl. Cover with clingfilm and chill for 2 hours.

2 To assemble the salad, divide the tomato slices between 4–6 individual plates. Toss the smoked chicken, watercress, beansprouts and parsley leaves together. Divide the salad ingredients between the plates.

3 Adjust the seasoning in the dressing, if necessary. Spoon the dressing over each salad and serve.

roast chicken with pesto cream salad

serves 4–6

- 600 g/1 lb 5 oz boneless cooked chicken, any skin removed and cut into bite-sized pieces
- 3 celery sticks, chopped
- 2 large skinned red peppers from a jar, well drained and sliced
- salt and pepper
- iceberg lettuce leaves, to serve

pesto cream

- 150 ml/5 fl oz crème fraîche or soured cream
- about 4 tbsp bottled pesto sauce

1 To make the pesto cream, put the crème fraîche into a large bowl, then beat in the pesto sauce. Taste and add more pesto if you want a stronger flavour.

2 Add the chicken, celery and red peppers to the bowl and gently toss together. Add salt and pepper to taste and toss again. Cover and chill until required.

3 Remove the salad from the fridge 10 minutes before serving to return to room temperature. Give the salad ingredients a good stir, then divide between individual plates lined with lettuce leaves and serve.

chicken & pancetta caesar salad

serves 2

- 12 thin smoked pancetta slices
- 225 g/8 oz skinless, boneless chicken breasts, cubed
- 1 garlic clove, crushed
- 3 tbsp olive oil
- 1 small rustic or ciabatta roll, cut into chunky cubes
- 1 small cos lettuce, chopped into large pieces
- fresh Parmesan cheese shavings, to serve

dressing

- 3 tbsp mayonnaise
- 2 tbsp soured cream
- 1 tbsp milk
- 1 garlic clove, crushed
- ½ tsp Dijon mustard
- 2 tbsp finely grated Parmesan cheese
- 2 anchovy fillets in oil, drained and finely chopped
- pepper

1 To make the dressing, place all the ingredients in a food processor or hand blender and process until smooth.

2 Heat a large non-stick frying pan and add the pancetta slices. Cook over a high heat for about 2 minutes until crisp and frazzled. Remove with a slotted spoon and drain on kitchen paper. Add the chicken to the pan and fry over a medium–high heat for 5–6 minutes until golden and cooked through. Remove and drain with the pancetta.

3 Add the garlic and oil to the pan and stir in the bread cubes. Fry over a high heat, turning frequently, for 2–3 minutes until crisp and golden.

4 Place the lettuce and dressing in a serving bowl and toss together thoroughly. Add the pancetta and chicken and toss in gently. Scatter over the garlic croûtons and Parmesan cheese shavings and serve immediately.

honey & chicken pasta salad

serves 4
- 250 g/9 oz dried fusilli
- 2 tbsp olive oil
- 1 onion, thinly sliced
- 1 garlic clove, crushed
- 400 g/14 oz skinless, boneless chicken breast, thinly sliced
- 2 tbsp wholegrain mustard
- 2 tbsp clear honey
- 175 g/6 oz cherry tomatoes, halved
- handful of mizuna or rocket leaves
- salt
- fresh thyme leaves, to garnish

dressing
- 3 tbsp olive oil
- 1 tbsp sherry vinegar
- 2 tsp clear honey
- 1 tbsp fresh thyme leaves
- salt and pepper

1 To make the dressing, place all the ingredients in a small bowl and whisk together.

2 Bring a large saucepan of lightly salted water to the boil. Add the pasta and return to the boil. Cook for 10–12 minutes until just tender.

3 Meanwhile, heat the oil in a large frying pan. Add the onion and garlic and fry for 5 minutes. Add the chicken and cook, stirring frequently, for 3–4 minutes until just cooked through. Stir the mustard and honey into the pan and cook for a further 2–3 minutes until the chicken and onion are golden brown and sticky.

4 Drain the pasta and transfer to a serving bowl. Pour over the dressing and toss well. Stir in the chicken and onion and leave to cool.

5 Gently stir the tomatoes and mizuna into the pasta. Serve garnished with the thyme leaves.

chicken & cranberry salad

serves 4

- 1 smoked chicken, weighing 1.3 kg/3 lb
- 115 g/4 oz dried cranberries
- 2 tbsp apple juice or water
- 200 g/7 oz mangetout
- 4 lettuce hearts
- 2 ripe avocados, peeled, stoned and sliced
- 1 bunch watercress, trimmed
- small handful of rocket leaves

dressing

- 2 tbsp olive oil
- 1 tbsp walnut oil
- 2 tbsp lemon juice
- 1 tbsp chopped fresh mixed herbs, such as parsley and lemon thyme
- salt and pepper

1 Carve the chicken carefully, slicing the white meat. Divide the legs into thighs and drumsticks and trim the wings. Cover with clingfilm and refrigerate. Put the cranberries in a bowl. Stir in the apple juice, cover with clingfilm and leave to soak for 30 minutes.

2 Meanwhile, blanch the mangetout, refresh under cold running water and drain. Separate the lettuce hearts and arrange on a large serving platter with the avocados, mangetout, watercress, rocket and the chicken.

3 To make the dressing, put all the ingredients into a small screw-top jar and shake until well blended. Drain the cranberries and mix them with the dressing, then pour over the salad. Serve immediately.

chicken & grapefruit salad

serves 4

- 2 skinless, boneless chicken breasts, about 175 g/6 oz each
- 1 bouquet garni
- few black peppercorns
- 2 pink grapefruit
- 3 Little Gem lettuces, separated into leaves
- 1 head chicory, separated into leaves
- fresh chervil sprigs, to garnish

dressing

- 1 tbsp light olive oil
- 3 tbsp Greek yogurt
- 1 tsp wholegrain mustard
- pinch of sugar
- 1 tbsp chopped fresh chervil
- salt and pepper

1 Place the chicken in a large saucepan and pour over enough water to cover. Add the bouquet garni and peppercorns and bring to a gentle simmer. Cover and simmer for 25–30 minutes until just cooked through. Leave the chicken to cool in the liquid.

2 Using a serrated knife, cut away the peel and pith from the grapefruit. Holding the fruit over a bowl to catch any juice, segment the flesh. Reserve 2 tablespoons of the juice.

3 Toss the salad leaves in a bowl with the grapefruit segments.

4 To make the dressing, place all the ingredients in a small bowl with the reserved grapefruit juice. Whisk together until thoroughly blended.

5 Drain the poached chicken and pat dry with kitchen paper. Tear into bite-sized strips or thinly slice. Arrange on top of the salad. Drizzle over the dressing and garnish with chervil sprigs.

chicken avocado salad

serves 4

- 125 g/4½ oz mixed salad leaves, such as beetroot greens, escarole, endive and radicchio, rinsed and dried
- 400 g/14 oz boneless cooked chicken, shredded
- 2 satsumas, separated into segments
- 2 celery sticks, thinly sliced
- ½ red onion, halved and thinly sliced
- 2 tbsp snipped fresh chives
- 2 avocados
- toasted sunflower seeds, to garnish
- pitta crisps, to serve

dressing

- 125 ml/4 fl oz extra virgin olive oil
- 3 tbsp Chinese rice wine vinegar
- ½ tsp Dijon mustard
- salt and pepper

1 To make the dressing, put all the ingredients into a small screw-top jar and shake until well blended.

2 Put the salad leaves into a bowl, add about one third of the dressing and lightly toss. Add the chicken, satsumas, celery, onion, chives and the remaining dressing and toss again.

3 Cut the avocados in half and remove the stone, then peel away the skin. Cut the flesh into thin slices, add to the other ingredients and gently toss together, making sure the avocado slices are completely coated with dressing so they don't discolour.

4 Arrange on individual plates, sprinkle with sunflower seeds and serve with pitta crisps on the side.

cajun chicken salad

serves 4

- 4 skinless, boneless chicken breasts, about 140 g/5 oz each
- 4 tsp Cajun seasoning
- 2 tsp sunflower oil (optional)
- 1 ripe mango, peeled, stoned and cut into thick slices
- 200 g/7 oz mixed salad leaves
- 1 red onion, cut in half and thinly sliced
- 175 g/6 oz cooked beetroot, diced
- 85 g/3 oz radishes, sliced
- 55 g/2 oz walnut halves
- sesame seeds, to garnish

dressing

- 4 tbsp walnut oil
- 1–2 tsp Dijon mustard
- 1 tbsp lemon juice
- salt and pepper

1 Make 3 diagonal slashes across each chicken breast. Put the chicken into a shallow dish and sprinkle all over with the Cajun seasoning. Cover and refrigerate for at least 30 minutes.

2 When ready to cook, brush a griddle pan with the sunflower oil, if using. Heat over a high heat until very hot and a few drops of water sprinkled into the pan sizzle immediately. Add the chicken and cook for 7–8 minutes on each side, or until thoroughly cooked. If still slightly pink in the centre, cook a little longer. Remove the chicken and reserve.

3 Add the mango slices to the pan and cook for 2 minutes on each side. Remove and reserve.

4 Meanwhile, arrange the salad leaves in a salad bowl and scatter over the onion, beetroot, radishes and walnut halves.

5 To make the dressing, put all the ingredients into a small screw-top jar and shake until well blended. Pour over the salad.

6 Add the mango, top with the chicken breast and sprinkle with sesame seeds. Serve.

bbq chicken salad

serves 4
- 1 tbsp olive oil
- 4 tbsp tomato sauce
- 1 tbsp clear honey
- 1 tbsp Worcestershire sauce
- 1 tsp mustard powder
- 4 boneless chicken breasts (with skin), about 140 g/5 oz each
- 4 Little Gem lettuces, separated into leaves
- 4 carrots, roughly grated
- 6 tbsp canned sweetcorn, drained
- ½ red pepper, thinly sliced
- salt and pepper
- fresh chives, to garnish (optional)

dressing
- 6 tbsp soured cream
- 2 tbsp snipped fresh chives
- salt and pepper

1 Place the oil, tomato sauce, honey, Worcestershire sauce and mustard powder in a shallow bowl and mix together well. Season with salt and pepper. Add the chicken and turn to coat in the marinade. Cover and leave to marinate in the refrigerator for 3–4 hours or overnight.

2 Preheat the barbecue. Drain the chicken, reserving the marinade. Cook the chicken over medium-hot coals, turning frequently and brushing with the reserved marinade, until thoroughly cooked. Leave to cool.

3 Arrange the lettuce leaves, carrots, sweetcorn and red pepper on 4 serving plates. To make the dressing, mix the soured cream and chives in a small bowl and season with salt and pepper.

4 Thickly slice each chicken breast and arrange on the salads. Garnish with fresh chives, if using, and serve.

chicken fajita salad

serves 4

- 450 g/1 lb skinless, boneless chicken breasts, sliced
- 2 tbsp lime juice
- 2 tbsp olive oil
- 1 tsp pepper
- 1 tsp dried oregano
- 1 tsp mild chilli powder
- 1 onion, sliced into thin wedges
- 1 red pepper, deseeded and thickly sliced
- 200 g/7 oz mixed salad leaves
- lime slices and soured cream, to serve

avocado salsa

- 1 ripe avocado, finely diced
- 2 ripe tomatoes, finely chopped
- 1 tbsp fresh chopped coriander
- 1 tbsp lime juice
- salt and pepper

1 To make the avocado salsa, place the avocado in a small bowl and stir in the tomatoes, coriander and lime juice. Season with salt and pepper. Cover the surface closely with clingfilm and chill in the refrigerator.

2 Place the chicken in a bowl. Add the lime juice, oil, pepper, oregano and chilli powder. Toss to coat. Cover and leave to marinate at room temperature for 1 hour.

3 Heat a cast iron griddle pan until very hot and add the chicken slices. Cook for 5–6 minutes, turning occasionally, until the chicken is cooked through and charred in places. Remove from the pan and keep warm. Add the onion and red pepper to the pan and cook for 3–4 minutes, turning once until just tender.

4 Divide the salad leaves between 4 serving plates and top with the chicken, onion and red pepper. Serve immediately with the avocado salsa, lime slices and soured cream.

thai chicken salad

serves 6
- vegetable oil spray
- 115 g/4 oz skinless chicken breast, cut lengthways horizontally
- 25 g/1 oz rice vermicelli
- shop bought low-fat spicy dressing of your choice
- 3 limes, halved, for squeezing over

salad
- 50 g/1¾ oz deseeded mixed peppers, finely sliced into strips
- 50 g/1¾ oz carrots, finely sliced into strips
- 50 g/1¾ oz courgettes, finely sliced into strips
- 50 g/1¾ oz mangetout, finely sliced into strips
- 50 g/1¾ oz baby corn cobs, finely sliced into strips
- 50 g/1¾ oz broccoli florets, cut into 5-mm/¼-inch pieces
- 50 g/1¾ oz pak choi, shredded
- 4 tbsp roughly chopped fresh coriander

1 Heat a griddle pan over a high heat and spray lightly with oil. Add the chicken and cook for 2 minutes on each side, or until thoroughly cooked through. Remove the chicken from the pan and shred.

2 Cook the vermicelli according to the packet instructions.

3 To make the salad, put all the salad ingredients with the chicken into a large bowl. Drain the vermicelli and add to the bowl. Pour over enough dressing to coat the ingredients and toss together, making sure that all the ingredients are well coated.

4 Cover and refrigerate for at least 2 hours before serving. Serve on large plates, squeezing the juice from half a lime over each portion.

chinese chicken salad

serves 4

- 3 boneless, skinless chicken breasts, weighing 450 g/ 1 lb in total, cut into bite-sized pieces
- 2 tsp soy sauce
- ¼ tsp freshly ground white pepper
- 2 tbsp groundnut oil, plus extra for deep-frying
- 50 g/1¾ oz thin rice noodles
- ½ head Chinese leaves, thinly sliced diagonally
- 3 spring onions, green parts included, sliced diagonally
- 40 g/1½ oz almonds with skin, sliced lengthways
- sesame seeds, to garnish (optional)

dressing

- 5 tbsp olive oil
- 3 tbsp rice vinegar
- 3 tbsp soy sauce
- a few drops sesame oil
- salt and pepper

1 Sprinkle the chicken with the soy sauce and white pepper. To make the dressing, whisk the ingredients together in a bowl until well blended.

2 Heat a wok over a high heat, then add the groundnut oil. Stir-fry the chicken for 4–5 minutes until brown and crisp. Drain on kitchen paper and allow to cool. Wipe out the wok.

3 Pour enough groundnut oil for deep-frying into the wok. Heat to 180°C/350°F or until a cube of bread browns in 30 seconds, then fry a few noodles at a time until puffed up and crisp. Drain on kitchen paper.

4 Arrange the Chinese leaves in a shallow serving dish. Place the noodles in a pile on top of the leaves on one side of the dish. Arrange the chicken, spring onions and almonds in the remaining space. Whisk the dressing again and pour over the salad. Garnish with the sesame seeds, if using. Serve.

gingered chicken & vegetable salad

serves 4

- 4 skinless, boneless chicken breasts
- 4 spring onions, chopped
- 2.5-cm/1-inch piece fresh ginger, finely chopped
- 2 garlic cloves, crushed
- 2 tbsp vegetable oil or groundnut oil

salad

- 1 tbsp vegetable or groundnut oil
- 1 onion, sliced
- 2 garlic cloves, chopped
- 115 g/4 oz baby sweetcorn, halved
- 115 g/4 oz mangetout, halved lengthways
- 1 red pepper, deseeded and sliced
- 7.5-cm/3-inch piece cucumber, peeled, deseeded and sliced
- 4 tbsp Thai soy sauce
- 1 tbsp jaggery or soft light brown sugar
- a few fresh Thai basil leaves
- 175 g/6 oz fine egg noodles

1 Cut the chicken into 2.5-cm/1-inch pieces. Mix the spring onions, ginger, garlic and oil together in a shallow dish and add the chicken. Cover and marinate for at least 3 hours. Lift the meat out of the marinade and set aside.

2 Heat the oil in a wok, add the onion and cook for 1–2 minutes. Add the garlic and the rest of the vegetables, except the cucumber, and cook for 2–3 minutes until just tender. Add the cucumber, half the soy sauce, the sugar and the basil, and mix gently.

3 Soak the noodles for 2–3 minutes (check the packet instructions), or until tender, and drain well. Sprinkle the remaining soy sauce over them and arrange on plates. Top with the cooked vegetables.

4 Add a little more oil to the wok if necessary, add the chicken and cook over a fairly high heat until browned on all sides. Arrange the chicken on top of the salad and serve hot or warm.

turkey & peanut salad

serves 4

- 225 g/8 oz Chinese leaves, roughly torn
- 2 carrots, cut into thin sticks
- ½ cucumber, deseeded and cut into thin sticks
- 55 g/2 oz beansprouts
- 400 g/14 oz cooked boneless turkey breast, shredded
- 1 tbsp toasted sesame seeds
- 1 tbsp salted peanuts, chopped

dressing

- 4 tbsp smooth peanut butter
- 2 tbsp sweet chilli sauce
- 1 tbsp soy sauce
- 1 tbsp rice vinegar
- 1 tbsp sunflower oil
- 1 tbsp roasted peanut oil

1 To make the dressing, place the peanut butter in a heatproof bowl. Set the bowl over a saucepan of simmering water and stir until the peanut butter has melted. Stir in the chilli sauce, soy sauce and rice vinegar. Remove from the heat and gradually stir in the sunflower and peanut oil to make a dressing with a smooth pouring consistency.

2 Arrange the Chinese leaves on a serving platter and top with the carrots, cucumber and beansprouts. Top with the shredded turkey and spoon over the warm dressing. Sprinkle with the sesame seeds and peanuts and serve immediately.

turkey couscous salad

serves 4
- 225 g/ 8 oz couscous
- 5 tbsp olive oil
- 3 tbsp red wine vinegar
- 350 g/12 oz turkey breast fillet, cubed
- 1 tsp harissa paste
- 175 g/6 oz courgettes, diced
- 1 onion, chopped
- 115 g/4 oz ready-to-eat dried apricots, chopped
- 2 tbsp pine kernels, toasted
- 2 tbsp chopped fresh coriander
- salt and pepper
- fresh coriander sprigs, to garnish

1 Place the couscous in a large heatproof bowl. Pour over enough boiling water to cover. Stir well, cover and leave to soak for about 15 minutes until all the liquid has been absorbed. Use a fork to break up any clumps and stir in 3 tablespoons of the olive oil and the vinegar. Season with plenty of salt and pepper.

2 Heat the rest of the oil in a large frying pan and add the turkey and harissa paste. Fry for 3 minutes, turning frequently, until the turkey is no longer pink. Add the courgettes and onion to the pan and fry for a further 10–12 minutes, stirring occasionally, until the turkey and vegetables are golden brown and tender.

3 Stir the turkey and vegetables into the couscous with the apricots and pine kernels. Cool for 10 minutes then stir in the chopped coriander and adjust the seasoning to taste. Serve piled into bowls garnished with coriander sprigs.

turkey & rice salad

serves 4

- 1 litre/1¾ pints chicken stock
- 175 g/6 oz mixed long-grain and wild rice
- 2 tbsp sunflower or corn oil
- 225 g/8 oz skinless, boneless turkey breast, trimmed of all visible fat and cut into thin strips
- 225 g/8 oz mangetout
- 115 g/4 oz oyster mushrooms, torn into pieces
- 55 g/2 oz shelled pistachio nuts, finely chopped
- 2 tbsp chopped fresh coriander
- 1 tbsp snipped fresh garlic chives
- 1 tbsp balsamic vinegar
- salt and pepper
- fresh garlic chives, to garnish

1 Reserve 3 tablespoons of the chicken stock and bring the remainder to the boil in a large saucepan. Add the rice and cook for 30 minutes, or until tender. Drain and leave to cool slightly.

2 Meanwhile, heat 1 tablespoon of the oil in a preheated wok or frying pan. Stir-fry the turkey over a medium heat for 3–4 minutes, or until cooked through. Using a slotted spoon, transfer the turkey to a dish. Add the mangetout and mushrooms to the wok and stir-fry for 1 minute. Add the reserved stock, bring to the boil, then reduce the heat, cover and simmer for 3–4 minutes. Transfer the vegetables to the dish and leave to cool slightly.

3 Thoroughly mix the rice, turkey, mangetout, mushrooms, nuts, coriander and garlic chives together, then season to taste with salt and pepper. Drizzle with the remaining oil and the vinegar and garnish with fresh garlic chives. Serve warm.

turkey salad pittas

makes 2

- small handful baby leaf spinach, rinsed, patted dry and shredded
- ½ red pepper, deseeded and thinly sliced
- ½ carrot, peeled and roughly grated
- 4 tbsp hummus
- 85 g/3 oz boneless, skinless cooked turkey meat, thinly sliced
- ½ tbsp toasted sunflower seeds
- 1 wholemeal pitta bread
- salt and pepper

1 Preheat the grill to high. Put the spinach leaves, red pepper, carrot and hummus into a large bowl and stir together, so all the salad ingredients are coated with the hummus. Stir in the turkey and sunflower seeds and season with salt and pepper to taste.

2 Put the pitta bread under the grill for about 1 minute on each side to warm through, but do not brown. Cut it in half to make 2 'pockets' of bread.

3 Divide the salad between the bread pockets and serve.

roast duck salad

serves 4
- 2 duck breasts
- 2 Little Gem lettuces, shredded
- 115 g/4 oz beansprouts
- 1 yellow pepper, deseeded and cut into thin strips
- ½ cucumber, deseeded and cut into matchsticks
- shredded lime zest and shredded coconut, to garnish

dressing
- juice of 2 limes
- 3 tbsp Thai fish sauce
- 1 tbsp soft brown sugar
- 2 tsp sweet chilli sauce
- 2.5 cm/1 inch fresh ginger, grated
- 3 tbsp chopped fresh mint
- 3 tbsp chopped fresh basil

1 Preheat the oven to 200°C/400°F/Gas Mark 6. Place the duck breasts on a rack set over a roasting tin and roast in the oven for 20–30 minutes, or until cooked as desired and the skin is crisp. Remove from the oven and set aside to cool.

2 In a large bowl, combine the lettuces, beansprouts, yellow pepper and cucumber. Cut the cooled duck into slices and add to the salad. Mix well.

3 To make the dressing, whisk all the ingredients in a bowl. Add the dressing to the salad and toss well.

4 Turn the salad out onto a serving platter and garnish with the shredded lime zest and coconut before serving.

warm duck, shallot & orange salad

serves 4

- 2 large oranges
- 4 duck breast fillets, about 175 g/6 oz each
- 12 small shallots, halved
- 1 tbsp sugar
- 2 tbsp olive oil
- 1 tbsp red wine vinegar
- small handful of baby spinach leaves
- small handful of baby red chard leaves
- salt and pepper

1 Halve and squeeze the juice from 1 of the oranges. Using a serrated knife remove all the peel and white pith from the other orange and halve and thinly slice.

2 Preheat the oven to 200°C/400°F/Gas Mark 6. Season the duck fillets with salt and pepper. Heat a large heavy-based frying pan and add the duck fillets, skin side down. Cook over a medium–high heat for 5–6 minutes until the skin is golden brown. Turn over and cook for a further minute. Place the duck fillets in a shallow roasting tin and roast in the preheated oven for 10 minutes. Cook for a little longer if you prefer the duck well done.

3 Add the shallots to the pan and turn to coat in the duck fat. Fry gently for 7–8 minutes until golden and tender. Remove with a slotted spoon and keep warm. Pour the orange juice into the pan and bring to the boil. Whisk in the sugar, oil and vinegar and simmer for 2–3 minutes until just syrupy. Season to taste with salt and pepper.

4 Arrange the spinach, chard leaves and orange slices on 4 serving plates. Slice each duck fillet and place on top of the salad with the shallots. Spoon over the warm dressing and serve immediately.

duck & radish salad

serves 4
- 350 g/12 oz boneless duck breasts
- 2 tbsp plain flour
- 1 egg
- 2 tbsp water
- 2 tbsp sesame seeds
- 3 tbsp sesame oil
- ½ head Chinese leaves, shredded
- 3 celery sticks, finely sliced
- 8 radishes, trimmed and halved
- salt and pepper
- fresh basil leaves, to garnish

dressing
- finely grated rind of 1 lime
- 2 tbsp lime juice
- 2 tbsp olive oil
- 1 tbsp light soy sauce
- 1 tbsp chopped fresh basil
- salt and pepper

1 Put each duck breast between sheets of greaseproof paper or clingfilm. Use a meat mallet or rolling pin to beat them out and flatten them slightly. Sprinkle the flour onto a large plate and season with salt and pepper. Beat the egg and water together in a shallow bowl, then sprinkle the sesame seeds on to a separate plate.

2 Dip the duck breasts first into the seasoned flour, then into the egg mixture and finally into the sesame seeds, to coat the duck evenly. Heat the sesame oil in a preheated wok or large frying pan. Fry the duck breasts over a medium heat for about 8 minutes, turning once. To test whether they are cooked, insert a skewer into the thickest part – the juices should run clear. Lift them out and drain on kitchen paper.

3 To make the dressing for the salad, whisk together the lime rind and juice, olive oil, soy sauce and chopped basil. Season with a little salt and pepper. Arrange the Chinese leaves, celery and radishes on a serving plate. Slice the duck breasts thinly and place on top of the salad.

4 Drizzle with the dressing and garnish with fresh basil leaves. Serve immediately.

duck salad with sweet chilli dressing

serves 4

- 2 duck leg portions, about 175 g/6 oz each
- 300 ml/10 fl oz boiling water
- 1 tsp Chinese five-spice powder
- 175 g/6 oz mangetout
- 1 small iceberg lettuce, finely shredded
- 2 celery sticks, very thinly sliced
- 6 spring onions, finely shredded

dressing

- 1 tbsp sunflower oil
- 3 tbsp sweet chilli sauce
- 1 tbsp rice vinegar
- salt and pepper

1 Preheat the oven to 200°C/400°F/Gas Mark 6. Place the duck legs in a roasting tin and pour the boiling water over the skin. Drain off the water and pat the skins dry with kitchen paper.

2 Rub the Chinese five-spice powder into the duck skin. Roast the duck legs in the preheated oven for 1¼–1½ hours until cooked through with golden crispy skin. Cool for 10 minutes.

3 To make the dressing, place all the ingredients in a small bowl and whisk together.

4 Bring a small saucepan of water to the boil and add the mangetout. Cook for 2 minutes then drain and refresh under cold running water. Thinly slice the mangetout lengthways and place in a bowl with the lettuce, celery and nearly all the spring onions. Toss well to mix.

5 Peel off the crispy skin from the roast duck and cut into thin strips. Using 2 forks pull and shred all the duck flesh from the bones.

6 Arrange the salad on a platter and top with the shredded duck and crispy skin. Drizzle over the dressing and garnish with the rest of the spring onions. Serve immediately.

duck & noodle salad with peanut sauce

serves 3

- 2 carrots, peeled
- 2 celery sticks
- 1 cucumber
- three 140-g/5-oz duck breasts
- 350 g/12 oz rice noodles, cooked according to the instructions on the packet, rinsed and drained

peanut sauce

- 2 garlic cloves, crushed
- 2 tbsp dark brown sugar
- 2 tbsp peanut butter
- 2 tbsp coconut cream
- 2 tbsp soy sauce
- 2 tbsp rice vinegar
- 2 tbsp sesame oil
- ½ tsp pepper
- ½ tsp Chinese five-spice powder
- ½ tsp ground ginger

1 Preheat the grill to high. Cut the carrots, celery and cucumber into thin strips and set aside.

2 Grill the duck breasts for about 5 minutes on each side until cooked through. Leave to cool.

3 Meanwhile, heat all the ingredients for the peanut sauce in a small saucepan until combined and the sugar has dissolved completely. Stir until smooth.

4 Slice the duck breasts. Divide the noodles among 3 serving bowls. Place the reserved carrots, celery and cucumber on top of the noodles, arrange the duck slices on top and drizzle with the sauce. Serve immediately.

duck salad with plum & chilli

serves 4

- 175 g/6 oz duck breasts, trimmed of all visible fat
- 2–3 sprays sunflower oil
- 2.5-cm/1-inch piece fresh ginger, peeled and grated
- 1 fresh serrano chilli, deseeded and sliced
- 1 red onion, cut into thin wedges
- 2 celery sticks, trimmed and finely sliced
- 1 small red pepper, deseeded and finely sliced
- 1 tbsp soy sauce
- 115 g/4 oz courgettes, trimmed and sliced
- 2 ripe but still firm plums, stoned and sliced
- 85 g/3 oz pak choi, sliced
- 1 tbsp chopped fresh coriander

1 Cut the duck breast into thin strips and reserve. Heat a wok until very hot then spray with the oil and heat for 30 seconds. Add the ginger, chilli and duck strips and stir-fry for 1–2 minutes, or until the duck strips are browned.

2 Add the onion wedges and celery and red pepper slices and continue to stir-fry for 3 minutes.

3 Add the soy sauce, courgettes and plums to the wok and stir-fry for 2 minutes before stirring in the sliced pak choi and the chopped coriander. Stir-fry for a further minute then serve, divided equally between 4 bowls.

Mmmm...
fish &
seafood

niçoise pasta salad

serves 4

- 350 g/12 oz dried conchiglie
- 115 g/4 oz green beans
- 50 g/1¾ oz canned anchovy fillets, drained
- 2 tbsp milk
- 2 small crisp lettuces
- 3 large beef tomatoes
- 4 hard-boiled eggs
- 225 g/8 oz canned tuna, drained
- 115 g/4 oz stoned black olives
- salt

dressing

- 3 tbsp extra virgin olive oil
- 2 tbsp white wine vinegar
- 1 tsp wholegrain mustard
- salt and pepper

1 Bring a large pan of lightly salted water to the boil over a medium heat. Add the pasta and cook for 8–10 minutes, until tender but still firm to the bite. Drain and refresh in cold water.

2 Bring a small pan of lightly salted water to the boil over a medium heat. Add the green beans and cook for 10–12 minutes, or until tender but still firm to the bite. Drain, refresh in cold water, drain again and reserve.

3 Put the anchovies in a shallow bowl, pour over the milk and leave to stand for 10 minutes. Meanwhile, tear the lettuces into large pieces. Blanch the tomatoes in boiling water for 1–2 minutes, then drain, skin and roughly chop the flesh. Shell the eggs and cut into quarters. Flake the tuna into large chunks.

4 Drain the anchovies and the pasta. Put all the salad ingredients into a large bowl and gently mix together.

5 To make the dressing, beat together the oil, vinegar and mustard and season to taste with salt and pepper. Chill in the refrigerator until required. Just before serving, pour the dressing over the salad.

caramelized tuna salad

serves 4
- 175 g/6 oz fresh beansprouts
- 10 cm/4 inch piece of cucumber
- 20 g/¾ oz fresh coriander leaves
- 20 g/¾ oz fresh mint leaves
- 1 tsp sesame oil, plus a few drops for drizzling
- 1 tbsp groundnut oil
- 450 g/1 lb fresh tuna, cut into 2.5-cm/1-inch chunks
- salt
- 2 tbsp salted roasted peanuts, crushed, to garnish

dressing
- 2 tsp rapeseed oil
- 1 tsp finely chopped fresh ginger
- ½–1 small red chilli, deseeded and finely chopped
- 4 tbsp light soy sauce
- 1 tbsp Thai fish sauce
- 1 tbsp tamarind paste
- 6 tbsp soft brown sugar

1 To make the dressing, heat a small wok over high heat. Add the oil and fry the ginger and chilli for a few seconds. Add the soy sauce, fish sauce and tamarind paste. Stir for 30 seconds, then add the sugar and stir until dissolved. Remove the wok from the heat and set aside.

2 Rinse the beansprouts in boiling water and drain. Blot dry with kitchen paper. Peel the cucumber, halve lengthways and scoop out the seeds. Thinly slice the flesh diagonally.

3 Put the beansprouts, cucumber, coriander and mint leaves in a bowl. Season with a pinch of salt and a few drops of toasted sesame oil. Toss to combine, then divide between individual serving plates.

4 Heat a wok over a high heat, then add the groundnut and sesame oils. Quickly stir-fry the tuna, turning with tongs, until coloured on the outside but still slightly red in the middle. Arrange the tuna chunks on top of the salad.

5 Reheat the dressing, thinning with a spoonful of water if necessary, and pour over the tuna. Sprinkle with the crushed peanuts and serve at once.

tuna, lentil & potato salad

serves 4

- 200 g/7 oz Puy or brown lentils
- 2 tbsp olive oil, plus extra for brushing
- 300 g/10½ oz baby new potatoes
- 1 Little Gem lettuce
- 4 fresh tuna steaks, about 100 g/3½ oz each
- 12 small cherry tomatoes, halved
- 40 g/1½ oz rocket leaves
- salt and pepper

dressing

- 5 tbsp fruity olive oil
- 1 tbsp balsamic vinegar
- 2 tsp red wine vinegar
- 1 tsp smooth Dijon mustard
- 1 tsp soft light brown sugar

1 Cook the lentils in a saucepan of boiling water for 25 minutes, or until tender. Drain, tip into a bowl and stir in the oil.

2 Meanwhile, place the potatoes in a saucepan and cover with cold water. Bring to the boil, cover and simmer for 15 minutes, or until tender when pierced with a fork.

3 Break off the outer lettuce leaves and cut the heart into 8 evenly sized pieces. Arrange on 4 individual serving plates.

4 To make the dressing, put all the ingredients into a small screw-top jar and shake until well blended.

5 When the potatoes are nearly cooked, lightly brush a ridged griddle pan with oil and heat over a high heat. When very hot, add the tuna steaks and cook for 1½ minutes on each side to sear. Remove to a chopping board and cut each steak into 6 chunks.

6 Drain the potatoes and roughly chop any larger ones. Arrange with the lentils, tuna and tomatoes on the serving plates, sprinkle over the rocket leaves and spoon over the dressing. Serve immediately.

tuna & two-bean salad

serves 4
- 200 g/7 oz French beans
- 400 g/14 oz canned small white beans, such as haricot, rinsed and drained
- 4 spring onions, finely chopped
- 2 fresh tuna steaks, about 225 g/8 oz each and 2 cm/¾ inch thick
- olive oil, for brushing
- 250 g/9 oz cherry tomatoes, halved
- handful of lettuce leaves
- salt and pepper
- fresh mint and flat-leaf parsley sprigs, to garnish

dressing
- handful of fresh mint leaves, shredded
- handful of fresh flat-leaf parsley leaves, chopped
- 1 garlic clove, crushed
- 4 tbsp extra virgin olive oil
- 1 tbsp red wine vinegar
- salt and pepper

1 To make the dressing, put all the ingredients into a small screw-top jar and shake until well blended.

2 Bring a saucepan of lightly salted water to the boil. Add the French beans and cook for 3 minutes. Add the white beans and cook for a further 4 minutes until the French beans are tender-crisp and the white beans are heated through. Drain well and add to the bowl with the dressing and spring onions. Toss together.

3 To cook the tuna, heat a ridged griddle pan over a high heat. Lightly brush the tuna steaks with oil, then season to taste with salt and pepper. Cook the steaks for 2 minutes, then turn over and cook on the other side for a further 2 minutes for rare or up to 4 minutes for well done.

4 Remove the tuna from the griddle pan and leave to rest for 2 minutes, or alternatively leave until completely cool. When ready to serve, add the tomatoes to the bean mixture and toss lightly. Line a serving platter with lettuce leaves and pile on the bean salad. Place the tuna over the top. Serve warm or at room temperature, garnished with the herbs.

smoked salmon & rocket salad

serves 4
- 50 g/1¾ oz rocket leaves
- 1 tbsp chopped fresh flat-leaf parsley
- 2 spring onions, finely diced
- 2 large avocados
- 1 tbsp lemon juice
- 250 g/9 oz smoked salmon

dressing
- 150 ml/5 fl oz mayonnaise
- 2 tbsp lime juice
- finely grated rind of 1 lime
- 1 tbsp chopped fresh flat-leaf parsley, plus extra sprigs to garnish

1 Shred the rocket and arrange in 4 individual bowls. Scatter over the chopped parsley and spring onions.

2 Halve, peel and stone the avocados and cut into thin slices or small chunks. Brush with the lemon juice to prevent discoloration, then divide between the salad bowls. Mix together gently. Cut the smoked salmon into strips and scatter over the top.

3 To make the dressing, put the mayonnaise in a bowl, then add the lime juice, lime rind and chopped parsley. Mix together well. Spoon some of the dressing on top of each salad and garnish with parsley sprigs.

teriyaki salmon salad

serves 4

- 6 spring onions, finely shredded
- 4 salmon fillets (with skin), about 115 g/4 oz each
- 4 tbsp teriyaki sauce
- 225 g/8 oz thread egg noodles
- 2 tsp toasted sesame oil
- 1 tsp grated fresh ginger
- 1 green pepper, finely shredded
- 2 carrots, finely shredded
- 2 tbsp sesame seeds
- 2 tbsp rice vinegar
- salt and pepper
- lime wedges, to serve

1 Place half the shredded spring onions in a small bowl of cold water with a couple of ice cubes. Leave in the refrigerator for at least 1 hour until the spring onions are curly. Put the salmon fillets in a shallow dish and pour over the teriyaki sauce. Cover and leave to marinate at room temperature for 30 minutes.

2 Cook the noodles in a saucepan of boiling water for 4 minutes, or according to the instructions on the packet, until soft. Drain well and refresh under cold running water. Transfer to a bowl. Heat the oil in a wok and add the ginger, green pepper, carrots and remaining spring onions. Stir-fry for 1 minute. Add the sesame seeds and stir-fry for a further minute. Cool for 10 minutes then add to the noodles with the vinegar and toss well to mix. Season with salt and pepper.

3 Heat a non-stick frying pan and add the salmon fillets, skin side down. Cook for 1 minute on each side until browned. Pour in the teriyaki marinade. Reduce the heat and cook for a further 3–4 minutes on each side until just cooked through. Divide the noodle salad between 4 serving plates and top each with a salmon fillet. Drain the spring onion curls and pat dry on kitchen paper. Arrange on top of the salmon fillets and serve with lime wedges.

warm salmon & mango salad

serves 4

- 115 g/4 oz yellow or red cherry tomatoes
- 85 g/3 oz salmon fillets, skinned and cut into small cubes
- 1 large ripe mango (about 150 g/5½ oz peeled fruit), peeled and cut into small chunks
- 2 tbsp orange juice
- 1 tbsp soy sauce
- 115 g/4 oz mixed salad leaves
- ½ cucumber, trimmed and sliced into batons
- 6 spring onions, trimmed and chopped

dressing

- 4 tbsp low fat natural yogurt
- 1 tsp soy sauce
- 1 tbsp finely grated orange rind

1 Soak 4 wooden skewers in cold water for 30 minutes, then drain. Cut half the tomatoes in half and set aside. Thread the salmon with the whole tomatoes and half the mango chunks onto 4 kebab sticks. Mix the orange juice and soy sauce together in a small bowl and brush over the kebabs. Leave to marinate for 15 minutes, brushing with the remaining orange juice mixture at least once more.

2 Arrange the salad leaves on a serving platter with the reserved halved tomatoes, mango chunks, the cucumber batons and the spring onions.

3 Preheat the grill to high and line the grill rack with foil. To make the dressing, mix the yogurt, soy sauce and grated orange rind together in a small bowl and reserve.

4 Place the salmon kebabs on the grill rack, brush again with the marinade and grill for 5–7 minutes, or until the salmon is cooked. Turn the kebabs over halfway through cooking and brush with any remaining marinade.

5 Divide the prepared salad between 4 plates, top each with a kebab, and then drizzle with the dressing.

tomato, salmon & prawn salad

serves 4

- 115 g/4 oz cherry or baby plum tomatoes
- handful lettuce leaves
- 4 ripe tomatoes, roughly chopped
- 100 g/3½ oz smoked salmon
- 200 g/7 oz large cooked prawns
- pepper

dressing

- 1 tbsp Dijon mustard
- 2 tsp caster sugar
- 2 tsp red wine vinegar
- 2 tbsp medium olive oil
- few fresh dill sprigs, plus extra to garnish

1 Halve most of the cherry tomatoes. Place the lettuce leaves around the edge of a bowl and add all the tomatoes and cherry tomatoes. Using scissors, snip the smoked salmon into strips and scatter over the tomatoes, then add the prawns.

2 To make the dressing, mix the mustard, sugar, vinegar and oil together in a small bowl, then tear most of the dill sprigs into it. Mix well and pour over the salad. Toss well to coat the salad with the dressing. Snip the remaining dill over the top, season to taste with pepper and serve.

salt cod salad

Serves 4–6

- 400 g/14 oz dried salt cod in one piece
- 6 spring onions, thinly sliced on the diagonal
- 6 tbsp extra virgin olive oil
- 1 tbsp sherry vinegar
- 1 tbsp lemon juice
- 2 large red peppers, grilled, peeled, deseeded and very finely diced
- 12 large black olives, stoned and sliced
- 2 large, juicy tomatoes, thinly sliced, to serve
- 2 tbsp very finely chopped fresh parsley, to garnish
- salt and pepper

1 Place the dried salt cod in a large bowl, cover with cold water and leave to soak for at least 48 hours, changing the water occasionally.

2 Pat the salt cod very dry with kitchen paper and remove the skin and bones, then use your fingers to tear into fine shreds. Put in a large, non-metallic bowl with the spring onions, oil, vinegar and lemon juice and toss together. Season with pepper, cover and put in the refrigerator to marinate for 3 hours.

3 Stir in the peppers and olives. Taste and adjust the seasoning, if necessary, remembering that the cod and olives might be salty. Arrange the tomato slices on a large platter or individual plates and spoon the salad on top. Sprinkle with parsley and serve.

smoked trout & pear salad

serves 4

- 2 ripe red William pears, cored and sliced
- 1 tbsp lemon juice
- 3 heads chicory, trimmed and leaves separated
- 55 g/2 oz watercress, tough stalks removed
- 225 g/8 oz smoked trout fillets
- 85 g/3 oz seedless green grapes, halved

dressing

- 4 tbsp crème fraîche
- 1 tbsp milk
- 1 tsp creamed horseradish
- 2 tsp lemon juice
- salt and pepper

1 Toss the sliced pears in the lemon juice to prevent discoloration. Place in a serving dish with the chicory leaves and watercress.

2 Flake the smoked trout, removing any skin and fine bones. Scatter over the salad with the grapes.

3 To make the dressing, place the crème fraîche, milk, horseradish and lemon juice in a small bowl and whisk until smooth. Season to taste with salt and pepper. Drizzle the dressing over the salad just before serving. Season with a little more pepper.

sweet & sour fish salad

serves 4

- 225 g/8 oz trout fillets
- 225 g/8 oz white fish fillets (such as haddock or cod)
- 300 ml/10 fl oz water
- 1 stalk lemon grass
- 2 lime leaves
- 1 large red chilli
- 1 bunch spring onions, trimmed and shredded
- 115 g/4 oz fresh pineapple flesh, diced
- 1 small red pepper, deseeded and diced
- 1 bunch watercress, washed and trimmed
- fresh snipped chives, to garnish

dressing

- 1 tbsp sunflower oil
- 1 tbsp rice wine vinegar
- pinch of chilli powder
- 1 tsp clear honey
- salt and pepper

1 Rinse the fish, place in a frying pan and pour over the water. Bend the lemon grass in half to bruise it and add to the pan with the lime leaves. Prick the chilli with a fork and add to the pan. Bring to the boil and simmer for 7–8 minutes. Let cool.

2 Drain the fish fillets thoroughly, flake the flesh away from the skin and place in a bowl. Gently stir in the spring onions, pineapple and red pepper.

3 Arrange the washed watercress on 4 serving plates and spoon the cooked fish mixture on top.

4 To make the dressing, put all the ingredients into a small bowl and mix well. Spoon over the fish and serve garnished with chives.

spiced fish skewers & tomato salad

serves 4

- 450 g/1 lb cod loin or monkfish, cut into 2.5-cm/1-inch cubes
- 3 tbsp lime juice
- 4 tbsp sunflower oil
- 2 tsp mild chilli powder
- 1 tsp dried oregano
- 1 lemon, cut into 8 wedges
- 225 g/8 oz red cherry tomatoes, halved
- 225 g/8 oz yellow cherry tomatoes, halved
- ½ small onion, thinly sliced
- 2 tbsp roughly chopped fresh coriander
- ½ tsp sugar
- 1 tsp mild mustard
- salt and pepper

1 Place the fish cubes in a shallow bowl. Mix together 2 tablespoons of the lime juice and 2 tablespoons of the oil with the chilli powder and oregano. Season with salt and pepper and pour over the fish. Cover and leave to marinate at room temperature for 1 hour.

2 Preheat the grill to medium. Thread the fish and lemon wedges onto 8 metal skewers and cook the fish skewers for 8–10 minutes, turning occasionally, until just cooked.

3 Meanwhile, mix together the tomatoes, onion and coriander in a bowl. Whisk the remaining lime juice and oil together with the sugar and mustard. Pour the dressing over the tomatoes and toss well to mix. Season with salt and pepper.

4 Divide the tomato salad between 4 serving dishes and top each with two fish skewers. Serve immediately.

seared swordfish with salsa

serves 4
- 4 boneless swordfish steaks, about 140 g/5 oz each
- knob of butter
- 1 tbsp olive oil
- salt
- fresh crusty bread, to serve

tomato & olive salsa
- 4 tbsp extra virgin olive oil
- 1 tbsp red wine vinegar
- 600 g/1 lb 5 oz ripe, juicy beef tomatoes, cored, deseeded and finely chopped
- 140 g/5 oz large black olives, stoned and cut in half
- 1 shallot, finely chopped or thinly sliced
- 1 tbsp capers in brine, rinsed and dried
- 3 tbsp finely shredded fresh basil leaves
- salt and pepper

1 To make the tomato and olive salsa, whisk the olive oil and vinegar together in a bowl large enough to hold all the ingredients. Gently stir in the tomatoes, olives, shallot and capers with salt and pepper to taste. Cover and chill until required.

2 Season the swordfish steaks on both sides with salt. Melt the butter with the oil in a frying pan large enough to hold the swordfish steaks in a single layer. (If you don't have a large enough pan, cook the steaks in 2 batches.)

3 Add the swordfish steaks to the pan in a single layer and fry for 5 minutes, or until golden brown, then carefully turn the fish over and continue frying about 3 minutes longer until the fish is cooked through and flakes easily. Remove the fish from the pan and set aside to cool completely. Cover and chill for at least 2 hours.

4 When ready to serve, remove the fish from the fridge at least 15 minutes in advance. Stir the basil into the salsa, then adjust the seasoning if necessary. Break the swordfish into large flakes and gently stir into the salsa – take care not to break up the fish too much. Arrange the fish salad in 4 bowls, spooning over any of the leftover juices and serve with slices of crusty bread.

warm mackerel & potato salad

serves 4

- 4 mackerel fillets, about 140 g/5 oz each
- 1 tsp coarsely ground black pepper
- 1 small lemon, finely pared rind and juice
- 1 tbsp virgin olive oil
- 450 g/1 lb new potatoes, sliced
- 4 spring onions, thinly sliced
- 25 g/1 oz rocket leaves
- fresh dill sprigs, to garnish

dressing

- 5 tbsp virgin olive oil
- 2 tbsp white wine vinegar
- 1 tsp Dijon mustard
- pinch of sugar
- 1 tbsp chopped fresh dill
- salt and pepper

1 Make 3–4 diagonal slashes in the skin of each mackerel fillet. Mix together the coarsely ground pepper, lemon rind and juice and oil and pour over the fillets. Cover and leave to marinate at room temperature for 20 minutes. Preheat the grill to high.

2 Cook the mackerel fillets under the grill for 7–8 minutes, turning once, until just cooked through. Meanwhile, place the potatoes in a saucepan and cover with cold water. Bring to the boil, cover and simmer for 12–15 minutes, or until tender when pierced with a fork.

3 To make the dressing, whisk the olive oil, vinegar, mustard and sugar together in a bowl until well blended. Stir in the dill and season to taste with salt and pepper.

4 Drain the potatoes and mix gently with the spring onions and half the dressing. Arrange on 4 serving plates and scatter over the rocket leaves. Top each salad with a hot mackerel fillet and drizzle over the rest of the dressing. Garnish with fresh dill sprigs and serve.

anchovy & olive salad

serves 4
- 125 g/4½ oz mixed lettuce leaves
- 12 cherry tomatoes, halved
- 20 black olives, stoned and halved
- 6 canned anchovy fillets, drained and thinly sliced
- 1 tbsp chopped fresh oregano
- lemon wedges, to garnish
- fresh crusty bread rolls, to serve

dressing
- 4 tbsp extra virgin olive oil
- 1 tbsp white wine vinegar
- 1 tbsp lemon juice
- 1 tbsp chopped fresh flat-leaf parsley
- salt and pepper

1 To make the dressing, put all the ingredients into a small bowl and stir together well.

2 To assemble the salad, arrange the lettuce leaves in a serving dish. Scatter the cherry tomatoes on top, followed by the olives, anchovies and oregano. Drizzle the dressing over the top.

3 Transfer to individual plates, garnish with lemon wedges and serve with crusty bread rolls.

prawn & white bean salad

serves 4

- 400 g/14 oz can haricot beans, drained and rinsed
- ½ red onion, finely chopped
- 1 celery stick, finely diced
- 300 g/10½ oz cooked, large peeled prawns with tails intact
- 1 garlic clove, finely chopped
- juice of 1 lemon
- 5 tbsp extra virgin olive oil
- 2 tbsp chopped fresh flat-leaf parsley
- 4 thick slices country bread (pain de campagne)
- 85 g/3 oz baby plum tomatoes, halved
- handful of fresh flat-leaf parsley leaves
- salt and pepper

1 Place the beans, onion, celery, prawns and garlic in a large shallow bowl. Add the lemon juice, 2 tablespoons of the oil and the chopped parsley. Season lightly with salt and pepper. Stir well then cover and set aside.

2 Brush the slices of bread with some of the remaining olive oil. Cook on a hot griddle for 2–3 minutes on each side until golden or toast under a hot grill. Place on 4 serving plates.

3 Gently stir the tomatoes and parsley leaves into the salad. Pile the salad onto the hot toasts. Drizzle over the rest of the olive oil, season with a little more pepper and serve.

prawn & rice salad

serves 4
- 175 g/6 oz mixed long-grain and wild rice
- 350 g/12 oz cooked, peeled prawns
- 1 mango, peeled, stoned and diced
- 4 spring onions, sliced
- 25 g/1 oz flaked almonds
- 1 tbsp finely chopped fresh mint
- salt and pepper

dressing
- 1 tbsp extra virgin olive oil
- 2 tsp lime juice
- 1 garlic clove, crushed
- 1 tsp clear honey
- salt and pepper

1 Cook the rice in a large saucepan of lightly salted boiling water for 35 minutes, or until tender. Drain and transfer to a large bowl, then add the prawns.

2 To make the dressing, mix all the ingredients together in a large jug, seasoning to taste with the salt and pepper, and whisk well until thoroughly blended. Pour the dressing over the rice and prawn mixture and leave to cool.

3 Add the mango, spring onions, almonds and mint to the salad and season to taste with pepper. Stir thoroughly and transfer to a large serving dish and serve.

coconut & prawn salad

serves 4
- 200 g/7 oz brown basmati rice
- ½ tsp coriander seeds
- 2 egg whites, lightly beaten
- 100 g/3½ oz unsweetened desiccated coconut
- 24 raw tiger prawns, peeled
- ½ cucumber
- 4 spring onions, thinly sliced lengthways
- 1 tsp sesame oil
- 1 tbsp finely chopped fresh coriander

1 Bring a large saucepan of water to the boil, add the rice and cook for 25 minutes, or until tender. Drain and keep in a colander covered with a clean tea towel to absorb the steam. Meanwhile, soak 8 wooden skewers in cold water for 30 minutes, then drain. Crush the coriander seeds in a mortar with a pestle. Heat a non-stick frying pan over a medium heat, add the crushed coriander seeds and cook, turning, until they begin to colour. Tip onto a plate and set aside.

2 Put the egg whites into a shallow bowl and the coconut into a separate bowl. Roll each prawn first in the egg whites, then in the coconut. Thread onto a skewer. Repeat so that each skewer is threaded with 3 coated prawns. Preheat the grill to high. Using a potato peeler, peel long strips from the cucumber to create ribbons, put into a colander to drain, then toss with the spring onions and oil in a bowl and set aside.

3 Cook the prawns under the preheated grill for 3–4 minutes on each side, or until slightly browned. Meanwhile, mix the rice with the toasted coriander seeds and fresh coriander and divide this and the cucumber salad between bowls. Serve with the hot prawn skewers.

thai crab patty salad

serves 4
- 2 x 175 g/6 oz cans white crabmeat, drained
- 140 g/5 oz cooked peeled prawns
- 1 tsp lime juice
- 2 tsp Thai red curry paste
- 1 tbsp beaten egg white
- 1 tbsp chopped fresh coriander
- flour, for dusting
- sunflower oil, for shallow frying
- ½ cucumber, peeled, deseeded and thinly sliced
- 225 g/8 oz beansprouts
- 25 g/1 oz salad cress
- 2 tbsp chopped fresh coriander stalks
- 1 tbsp rice vinegar
- 4 tbsp sweet chilli sauce
- salt and pepper
- lime wedges, to garnish

1 Place the crab, prawns, lime juice and curry paste in a food processor and process for a few seconds until finely minced. Add the egg white and chopped coriander and season well with salt and pepper. Process for a further few seconds until well mixed.

2 Transfer the mixture to a bowl and using lightly floured hands, shape into 12 small cakes. Coat lightly in the flour. Cover and chill in the refrigerator for 1 hour.

3 Heat the oil in a large frying pan and fry the crab cakes, in 2 batches, for 3–4 minutes until golden brown, turning once. Drain on kitchen paper.

4 Place the cucumber, beansprouts, salad cress and coriander stalks in a bowl and toss together with the rice vinegar. Divide between 4 serving plates. Top with the hot crabcakes and spoon over the chilli sauce. Serve garnished with lime wedges.

spicy warm crab salad

serves 4

- 2 sprays sunflower oil
- 1 fresh serrano chilli, deseeded and finely chopped
- 115 g/4 oz mangetout, cut in half diagonally
- 6 spring onions, trimmed and finely shredded
- 25 g/1 oz frozen sweetcorn kernels, defrosted
- 150 g/5½ oz white crabmeat, drained if canned
- 55 g/2 oz raw prawns, peeled and deveined, thawed if frozen
- 1 carrot, about 85 g/3 oz, peeled and grated
- 115 g/4 oz beansprouts
- 225 g/8 oz fresh baby spinach leaves
- 1 tbsp finely grated orange rind
- 2 tbsp orange juice
- chopped fresh coriander, to garnish

1 Heat a wok and when hot, spray in the oil and heat for 30 seconds. Add the chilli and mangetout then stir-fry over a medium heat for 2 minutes.

2 Add the spring onions and sweetcorn and continue to stir-fry for a further 1 minute.

3 Add the crabmeat, prawns, grated carrot, beansprouts and spinach leaves. Stir in the orange rind and juice and stir-fry for 2–3 minutes, or until the spinach has begun to wilt and everything is cooked through. Serve divided between 4 bowls, sprinkled with the chopped coriander.

lobster & summer herb salad

serves 4-6

- 750–800 g/1 lb 10 oz–1 lb 12 oz freshly cooked lobster meat, cut into bite-sized chunks
- 1 large avocado, peeled, stoned and cut into chunky dice
- 4 ripe but firm tomatoes
- 250 g/9 oz mixed herb salad leaves
- 1–2 tbsp fruity olive oil
- squeeze of lemon juice
- salt and pepper

saffron mayonnaise

- pinch of saffron threads
- 1 egg
- 1 tsp Dijon mustard
- 1 tbsp white wine vinegar
- pinch of salt
- 300 ml/10 fl oz sunflower oil
- salt and pepper

1 To make the saffron mayonnaise, soak the saffron threads in a little warm water. Meanwhile, put the egg, mustard, vinegar and salt in a blender and whiz to combine. With the motor running, slowly trickle in about one third of the sunflower oil. Once the mixture starts to thicken, add the remaining oil more quickly. When all the oil has been incorporated, add the saffron and its soaking water and whiz to combine. Add more salt, and pepper, to taste, cover and refrigerate until required.

2 Put the lobster meat and avocado in a bowl. Quarter the tomatoes and remove the seeds. Cut the flesh into fairly chunky dice and add to the bowl. Season the lobster mixture to taste with salt and pepper and gently stir in enough of the mayonnaise to give everything a light coating. Toss the salad leaves with the olive oil and lemon juice. Divide between four to six plates and top with the lobster mixture. Serve immediately.

layered crayfish salad

serves 4

- 115 g/4 oz carrots, peeled and grated
- 1 Little Gem lettuce, shredded
- 85 g/3 oz canned sweetcorn kernels, drained
- ¼ cucumber, diced
- 175 g/6 oz cooked crayfish tails in brine, thoroughly drained
- ½ tsp cayenne pepper
- lemon wedges, to garnish (optional)

dressing

- 8 tbsp mayonnaise
- 1 tbsp tomato ketchup
- dash of Worcestershire sauce
- 1 tbsp lemon juice
- salt and pepper

1 To make the dressing, put all the ingredients into a small bowl and mix well.

2 Divide the grated carrot, lettuce, sweetcorn and cucumber between four bowls.

3 Spoon over the dressing and pile the crayfish tails on top. Sprinkle with the cayenne pepper. Garnish with lemon wedges, if using, and serve.

squid, watercress & baby spinach salad

serves 4

- 12 squid tubes and tentacles (about 700 g/1 lb 9 oz total weight), cleaned and prepared
- 2–3 tbsp olive oil
- 1–2 red chillies, deseeded and thinly sliced
- 2 spring onions, finely chopped
- lemon wedges, for squeezing and to serve
- 115 g/4 oz watercress
- 85 g/3 oz baby spinach leaves or rocket leaves
- salt and pepper

dressing

- 100 ml/3½ fl oz olive oil
- juice of 1 lime
- 1 tsp caster sugar
- 2 shallots, thinly sliced
- 1 tomato, peeled, deseeded and finely chopped
- 1 garlic clove, crushed
- salt and pepper

1 To make the dressing, mix all the ingredients together in a bowl, season with salt and pepper to taste, cover and refrigerate until required.

2 Cut the squid tubes into 5-cm/2-inch pieces, then score diamond patterns lightly across the flesh with the tip of a sharp knife. Heat the oil in a wok or large frying pan over a high heat, add the squid pieces and tentacles and stir-fry for 1 minute. Add the chillies and spring onions and stir-fry for a further minute. Season to taste with salt and pepper and add a good squeeze of lemon juice.

3 Mix the watercress and spinach together, then toss with enough of the dressing to coat lightly. Serve immediately with the squid, together with lemon wedges to squeeze over the squid and the remaining dressing.

mixed seafood salad

serves 4–6

- 2 garlic cloves, crushed
- juice of 1½ lemons
- 4 tbsp extra virgin olive oil
- 2 tbsp chopped fresh
  flat-leaf parsley
- 600 g/1 lb 5 oz cooked
  seafood cocktail (prawns,
  mussels, clams, calamari
  rings, cockles)
- 1 oil-cured roasted red
  pepper, sliced into thin strips
- 12 stoned black olives
- 2 tbsp fresh basil, to garnish
- salt and pepper

1 Whisk the garlic, lemon juice, oil and parsley with salt and pepper to taste.

2 Drain the seafood if necessary, and tip into a serving dish. Add the red pepper and olives, then mix with the garlic mixture, turning to coat. Leave in a cool place for 30 minutes to allow the flavours to develop.

3 Stir again before serving, check the seasoning and sprinkle with the basil.

Mmmm...
vegetables
& pulses

goat's cheese croûton & spinach salad

serves 2

- 6 thin slices French bread
- 1 tbsp olive oil
- 115 g/4 oz round goat's cheese (with rind)
- 85 g/3 oz baby spinach leaves
- 55 g/2 oz sun blush tomatoes, drained
- pepper
- crusty bread, to serve

dressing

- 3 tbsp extra virgin olive oil
- 1 tbsp sherry vinegar
- 1 tsp wholegrain mustard
- pinch of sugar
- salt and pepper

1 To make the dressing, put all the ingredients into a small screw-top jar and shake until well blended.

2 Preheat the grill to medium. Lightly brush the slices of French bread with olive oil. Toast the rounds for 1–2 minutes on each side until just golden. Top each with a slice of goat's cheese, season with pepper and grill for a further 1–2 minutes until the cheese has melted.

3 Meanwhile, place the spinach in a large bowl. Add nearly all the dressing and toss gently to coat the leaves. Divide between 2 serving plates. Add the sun blush tomatoes and top with the cheese croûtons. Drizzle over the rest of the dressing and serve immediately with crusty bread.

lentil & goat's cheese salad

serves 1

- 25 g/1 oz dried Puy lentils
- 1 bay leaf
- 2 spring onions, finely chopped
- 50 g /1¾ oz red pepper, diced
- 15 ml/1 tbsp chopped fresh parsley
- 100 g/3½ oz cherry tomatoes, sliced in half
- 50 g/1¾ oz rocket
- 30 g/1 oz goat's cheese, sliced or crumbled, to serve

dressing

- 5 ml/1 tsp olive oil
- 5 ml/1 tsp balsamic vinegar
- 2.5 ml/½ tsp runny honey
- 1 clove garlic, peeled and crushed or finely chopped

1 Rinse the lentils and put in a medium-sized saucepan. Add the bay leaf and cover with plenty of cold water. Bring to the boil then reduce the heat and simmer for 20–30 minutes or until the lentils are tender.

2 Drain the lentils, discarding the bay leaf and transfer to a bowl. Add the spring onions, red pepper, parsley and cherry tomatoes. Mix well.

3 To make the dressing, whisk together the oil, vinegar, honey and garlic and stir into the lentils. Serve on a bed of rocket, with the goat's cheese sprinkled over.

bean salad with feta

serves 4
- 350 g/12 oz French beans, trimmed
- 1 red onion, chopped
- 3–4 tbsp chopped fresh coriander
- 2 radishes, thinly sliced
- 75 g/2¾ oz feta cheese, drained and crumbled
- 1 tsp chopped fresh oregano or ½ tsp dried oregano
- 2 tbsp red wine vinegar or fruit vinegar
- 5 tbsp extra virgin olive oil
- 3 ripe tomatoes, cut into wedges
- pepper

1 Place the beans in a saucepan and cover with cold water. Bring to the boil, cover and simmer for 5 minutes, or until tender when pierced with a fork. Drain and halve.

2 Transfer the beans to a bowl and add the onion, coriander, radishes and cheese.

3 Sprinkle the oregano over the salad, then grind pepper over to taste. Whisk the vinegar and olive oil together and pour over the salad. Toss gently to mix well.

4 Transfer to a serving platter, add the tomato wedges and serve at once or chill until ready to serve.

greek feta salad

serves 4

- handful vine leaves
- 4 tomatoes, sliced
- ½ cucumber, peeled and sliced
- 1 small red onion, sliced thinly
- 115 g/4 oz feta cheese, drained and cubed
- 8 black olives
- salt and pepper

dressing

- 3 tbsp extra virgin olive oil
- 1 tbsp lemon juice
- ½ tsp dried oregano
- salt and pepper

1 To make the dressing, put all the ingredients into a small screw-top jar and shake until well blended.

2 Arrange the vine leaves on a serving dish and then the tomatoes, cucumber and onion. Scatter the cheese and olives on top. Pour the dressing over the salad, season to taste with salt and pepper and serve.

strawberry & watercress salad

serves 4

- 115 g/4 oz watercress, tough stalks removed
- 350 g/12 oz strawberries, sliced
- 1 ripe avocado
- 1 tbsp lemon juice
- ¼ cucumber, finely diced
- 1 tbsp chopped walnuts
- salt and pepper

balsamic glaze

- 100 ml/3½ fl oz balsamic vinegar
- 2 tbsp sugar

1 To make the balsamic glaze, place the vinegar and sugar in a small saucepan. Heat gently, stirring, until the sugar dissolves. Simmer gently for 5–6 minutes until syrupy. Cool for 30 minutes.

2 Place the watercress in a serving dish and scatter over the strawberries. Halve, stone, peel and slice the avocado and toss gently in the lemon juice. Add to the salad. Scatter over the cucumber and walnuts.

3 Drizzle the glaze over the salad. Season lightly with salt and pepper and serve immediately.

feta, mint & strawberry salad

Serves 4–6

- 500 g/1 lb 2 oz fine green beans
- 500 g/1 lb 2 oz strawberries
- 2–3 tbsp pistachio nuts
- 1 small bunch fresh mint leaves
- 500 g/1 lb 2 oz feta cheese (drained weight)
- pepper

dressing

- 2 tbsp raspberry vinegar
- 2 tsp caster sugar
- 1 tbsp Dijon mustard
- pinch of salt
- 125 ml/4 fl oz olive oil

1 To make the dressing, mix the vinegar, sugar, mustard and salt together in a bowl until smooth. Slowly pour in the oil, whisking constantly until the mixture has emulsified. Cover and refrigerate until required.

2 Blanch the beans in a large saucepan of salted boiling water for 1–2 minutes, so that they retain plenty of crunch. Drain and quickly toss in a large, cool bowl. Hull and halve the strawberries, then add to the beans. Stir in the pistachio nuts and mint leaves. Toss the salad with enough of the dressing to coat lightly.

3 Break the feta cheese into chunks and scatter over the salad. Add a good grinding of pepper and serve immediately.

pear, rocket & blue cheese salad

Serves 4–6

- 1 dessert pear, such as Bosc
- 2 bunches wild rocket, rinsed and shaken dry
- 85 g/3 oz blue cheese, such as Gorgonzola, crumbled
- 3 tbsp pine kernels, toasted

dressing

- 4 tbsp extra virgin olive oil
- 1 tbsp balsamic vinegar
- salt and pepper

1 To make the dressing, put the oil, vinegar, and salt and pepper to taste in a large bowl and whisk until blended and thickened. Cover and set aside.

2 Just before serving, quarter, core and thinly slice the pear, adding it to the bowl with the dressing as it is prepared, then gently toss so all the pieces are coated with dressing. Add the rocket and cheese and toss again to combine. Sprinkle over the pine kernels and serve.

melon & grape with mixed salad leaves

serves 4

- 85 g/3 oz cottage cheese
- 1 tsp chopped fresh parsley
- 1 tbsp snipped fresh chives
- 1 tsp chopped fresh chervil or basil
- 2 assorted coloured peppers, deseeded and peeled
- 1 small melon, such as Ogen (about 300 g/ 10½ oz after peeling and deseeding)
- 175 g/6 oz assorted salad leaves
- 55 g/2 oz seedless grapes
- 1 red onion, thinly sliced

dressing

- 3 tbsp freshly squeezed lime juice
- 1 small fresh red chilli, deseeded and finely chopped
- 1 tsp clear honey
- 1 tbsp soy sauce

1 Place the cottage cheese in a bowl and stir in the chopped herbs. Cover lightly and reserve.

2 Cut the peeled peppers into thin strips and reserve. Cut the melon in half, discard the seeds and cut into small wedges.

3 Arrange the salad leaves on a large serving platter with the melon wedges.

4 Spoon the herb-flavoured cottage cheese on the platter and arrange the reserved peppers, grapes and red onion slices around the cheese.

5 To make the dressing, mix the lime juice, chilli, honey and soy sauce together in a small bowl or jug then drizzle over the salad and serve as 4 portions.

avocado, tomato & mozzarella salad

serves 4
- 2 tbsp pine kernels
- 175 g/6 oz dried fusilli
- 6 tomatoes
- 225 g/8 oz mozzarella cheese drained
- 1 large avocado
- 2 tbsp lemon juice
- 3 tbsp chopped fresh basil, plus extra sprigs to garnish
- salt and pepper

dressing
- 6 tbsp extra virgin olive oil
- 2 tbsp white wine vinegar
- 1 tsp wholegrain mustard
- pinch of sugar
- salt and pepper

1 Spread the pine kernels out on a baking tray and toast under a preheated hot grill for 1–2 minutes. Remove and leave to cool. Bring a large pan of lightly salted water to the boil over a medium heat. Add the pasta and cook for 8–10 minutes, or until tender but still firm to the bite. Drain the pasta and refresh in cold water. Drain again and leave to cool.

2 Thinly slice the tomatoes and the mozzarella cheese. Using a sharp knife, cut the avocado in half, remove the stone and skin, then cut into thin slices lengthways. Sprinkle with lemon juice to prevent discoloration. To make the dressing, whisk the oil, vinegar, mustard and sugar together in a small bowl. Season to taste with salt and pepper.

3 Arrange the sliced tomatoes, mozzarella cheese and avocado alternately in overlapping slices on a large serving platter. Toss the pasta with half the dressing and the chopped basil and season to taste with salt and pepper. Spoon the pasta onto the platter and pour over the remaining dressing. Sprinkle over the pine kernels and garnish with fresh basil sprigs. Serve immediately.

rocket & parmesan salad with pine kernels

serves 4

- 2 handfuls of rocket leaves
- 1 small fennel bulb
- 5 tbsp olive oil
- 2 tbsp balsamic vinegar
- 100 g/3½ oz Parmesan cheese
- 50 g/1¾ oz pine kernels
- salt and pepper

1 Wash the rocket, discarding any wilted leaves or coarse stems, and pat dry. Divide among 4 serving plates. Halve the fennel bulb and slice it finely. Arrange the sliced fennel over the rocket.

2 Whisk together the oil and vinegar with salt and pepper to taste. Drizzle a little of the dressing over each serving. Cut the Parmesan cheese into thin shavings using a knife or vegetable peeler.

3 Toast the pine kernels in a dry frying pan until golden brown. Top the salad with the Parmesan cheese shavings and toasted pine kernels. Serve immediately.

three - colour salad

serves 4
- 280 g/10 oz mozzarella cheese, drained
- 8 plum tomatoes
- 20 fresh basil leaves
- 125 ml/4 fl oz extra virgin olive oil
- salt and pepper

1 Cut the mozzarella into thin slices. Cut the tomatoes into thin slices.

2 Arrange the cheese and tomato slices on 4 individual serving plates and season to taste with salt. Set aside in a cool place for 30 minutes.

3 Sprinkle the basil leaves over the salad, then drizzle with the oil and season to taste with pepper. Serve immediately.

asparagus & tomato salad

serves 4
- 225 g/8 oz asparagus spears
- 1 lamb's lettuce, washed and torn
- 25 g/1 oz rocket or mizuna leaves
- 450 g/1 lb ripe tomatoes, sliced
- 12 black olives, stoned and chopped
- 1 tbsp pine kernels, toasted

dressing
- 1 tsp lemon oil
- 1 tbsp olive oil
- 1 tsp wholegrain mustard
- 2 tbsp balsamic vinegar
- salt and pepper

1 Steam the asparagus spears for about 8 minutes or until tender. Rinse under cold running water to prevent them cooking any further, then cut into 5-cm/2-inch pieces.

2 Arrange the lettuce and rocket leaves around a salad platter to form the base of the salad. Place the sliced tomatoes and asparagus on top. Add the olives and the pine kernels.

3 To make the dressing, put all the ingredients into a small screw-top jar and shake until well blended. Drizzle over the salad and serve.

watercress, mint & courgette salad

serves 4
- 2 courgettes, cut into batons
- 100 g/3½ oz French beans, cut into thirds
- 1 green pepper, deseeded and cut into strips
- 2 celery sticks, sliced
- 1 bunch watercress

dressing
- 200 ml/7 fl oz natural yogurt
- 1 garlic clove, crushed
- 2 tbsp chopped fresh mint
- pepper

1 Bring a large saucepan of water to the boil, add the courgette batons and beans and cook for 5 minutes, or until just tender. Remove with a slotted spoon and refresh the beans under cold running water. Set aside to cool completely.

2 Mix the courgettes and beans with the green pepper strips, celery and watercress in a large serving bowl.

3 To make the dressing, combine the yogurt, garlic and mint in a small bowl. Season with pepper to taste.

4 Spoon the dressing on to the salad and serve immediately.

minted pea
& melon salad

serves 4

- 350 g/12 oz wedge of watermelon
- ½ small honeydew melon
- ½ Charentais or cantaloupe melon
- ½ cucumber, peeled and diced
- 55 g/2 oz fresh pea shoots
- fresh mint leaves, to garnish

dressing

- 3 tbsp light olive oil
- 1 tbsp white wine vinegar
- ½ tsp caster sugar
- 1 tbsp chopped fresh mint
- salt and pepper

1 Cut all the melon flesh into even-sized chunks, removing any seeds. Place the chunks in a bowl with the cucumber.

2 To make the dressing, place all the ingredients in a small bowl and whisk together.

3 Pour the dressing over the melon and cucumber and toss well to coat. Cover and chill for 1 hour.

4 Add the pea shoots to the chilled melon and cucumber and gently toss together. Transfer to a serving bowl and serve garnished with mint leaves.

green & white bean salad

serves 4

- 100 g/3½ oz haricot beans, soaked overnight and drained
- 225 g/8 oz fine French beans, trimmed
- ¼ red onion, thinly sliced
- 12 stoned black olives
- 1 tbsp snipped fresh chives

dressing

- ½ tbsp lemon juice
- ½ tsp Dijon mustard
- 6 tbsp extra virgin olive oil
- salt and pepper

1 Place the haricot beans in a large saucepan. Cover with cold water and bring to the boil. Boil rapidly for 15 minutes, then reduce the heat and simmer for a further 30 minutes, or until tender. Drain and set aside.

2 Meanwhile, plunge the French beans into a large pan of boiling water. Bring back to the boil and cook for 4 minutes, until just tender but still brightly coloured. Drain and set aside.

3 Whisk together the dressing ingredients and season to taste with salt and pepper. Leave to stand. While both types of bean are still slightly warm, tip them into a shallow serving dish. Scatter over the onion, olives and chives.

4 Whisk the dressing again and spoon over the salad. Serve at room temperature.

red pepper & radicchio salad

serves 4

- 2 red peppers
- 1 head radicchio, separated into leaves
- 4 cooked whole beetroot, cut into matchsticks
- 12 radishes, sliced
- 4 spring onions, finely chopped
- 4 tbsp basic salad dressing
- fresh crusty bread, to serve

1 Core and deseed the peppers and cut into rounds.

2 Arrange the radicchio leaves in a salad bowl. Add the peppers, beetroot, radishes and spring onions. Drizzle with the dressing and serve with crusty bread.

marinated pepper salad

serves 4

- 2 red peppers
- 2 yellow peppers
- 1 red onion, roughly chopped
- 2 garlic cloves, chopped
- 6 tbsp olive oil
- 115 g/4 oz marinated black olives, drained
- 100 g/3½ oz mini mozzarella pearls, drained
- 2 tbsp roughly torn fresh basil leaves
- 2 tbsp balsamic vinegar
- salt and pepper

1 Preheat the oven to 190°C/375°F/Gas Mark 5. Halve the peppers, keeping the stalks on. Remove the white seeds and pith. Place the peppers, cut side up, in a shallow roasting tin. Scatter over the onion and garlic, season with salt and pepper and drizzle over half the olive oil. Roast for 40 minutes until the peppers are tender. Leave to cool.

2 Arrange the cold peppers on a serving plate and pour over any juices left in the roasting tin. Scatter over the olives, mozzarella pearls and basil.

3 Whisk together the remaining olive oil with the balsamic vinegar and pour over the peppers. Cover and leave to marinate in the refrigerator for at least 2 hours (or overnight) before serving.

pasta salad with peppers

serves 4
- 1 red pepper
- 1 orange pepper
- 280 g/10 oz dried conchiglie
- 5 tbsp extra virgin olive oil
- 2 tbsp lemon juice
- 2 tbsp bottled pesto sauce
- 1 garlic clove, finely chopped
- 3 tbsp shredded fresh basil leaves
- salt and pepper

1 Preheat the grill to high. Put the whole peppers on a baking sheet and place under the hot grill, turning frequently, for 15 minutes, or until charred all over. Remove with tongs and place in a bowl. Cover with crumpled kitchen paper and reserve.

2 Bring a large saucepan of lightly salted water to the boil. Add the pasta and return to the boil. Cook for 10–12 minutes until just tender.

3 Combine the olive oil, lemon juice, pesto sauce and garlic in a bowl, whisking well to mix. Drain the pasta, add it to the pesto mixture while still hot and toss well. Reserve until required.

4 When the peppers are cool enough to handle, peel off the skins, then cut open and remove the seeds. Chop the flesh roughly and add to the pasta with the basil. Season to taste with salt and pepper and toss well. Serve.

roasted vegetable salad

serves 4
- 1 onion
- 1 aubergine
- 1 red pepper, deseeded
- 1 orange pepper, deseeded
- 1 large courgette
- 2–4 garlic cloves
- 2–4 tbsp olive oil
- salt and pepper
- fresh basil leaves, to garnish
- fresh Parmesan cheese shavings and fresh crusty bread, to serve

dressing
- 1 tbsp balsamic vinegar
- 2 tbsp extra virgin olive oil

1 Preheat the oven to 200°C/400°F/Gas Mark 6. Cut all the vegetables into even-sized wedges, put into a roasting tin and scatter over the garlic.

2 Pour over 2 tablespoons of the olive oil and turn the vegetables in the oil until well coated. Add a little salt and pepper. Roast in the preheated oven for 40 minutes, or until tender, adding the extra olive oil if becoming too dry.

3 To make the dressing, put both ingredients into a small screw-top jar and shake until well blended.

4 Once the vegetables are cooked, remove from the oven, arrange on a serving dish and pour over the dressing. Garnish with the basil and serve with Parmesan cheese and crusty bread.

red cabbage & beetroot salad

serves 4
- 350 g/12 oz red cabbage, finely shredded
- 175 g/6 oz cooked beetroot, sliced into thin matchsticks
- 1 apple, cored and thinly sliced
- 1 tbsp lemon juice
- 1 tbsp sunflower seeds
- 1 tbsp pumpkin seeds
- salt and pepper

dressing
- 3 tbsp mayonnaise
- 2 tbsp Greek yogurt
- 1 tbsp red wine vinegar

1 Place the cabbage, beetroot and apple slices in a large bowl. Add the lemon juice and mix well.

2 To make the dressing, place the mayonnaise, yogurt and red wine vinegar in a bowl and mix together until smooth. Pour over the salad and stir well. Season with salt and pepper and cover and chill in the refrigerator for at least 1 hour.

3 Stir the salad thoroughly and adjust the seasoning to taste. Sprinkle with the sunflower and pumpkin seeds just before serving.

beetroot, fennel & avocado salad

Serves 4–6

- 2 avocados, halved, stoned and thinly sliced
- 2 fennel bulbs, trimmed and thinly sliced
- 2 golden, striped or ruby cooked beetroot, peeled and thinly sliced
- 2 tbsp snipped chives
- 2 tbsp fresh parsley, finely chopped
- 1 tbsp fresh basil, finely shredded
- 1 tbsp fresh mint, finely chopped
- 55 g/2 oz ricotta salata cheese, grated

dressing
- 125 ml/4 fl oz sunflower oil
- 2 tbsp fresh orange juice
- salt and pepper

1 To make the dressing, put the sunflower oil and orange juice in a large, non-metallic bowl and whisk until blended. Add salt and pepper to taste.

2 Add the avocado and fennel to the bowl and toss with your hands to coat in the dressing.

3 When ready to serve, arrange the beetroot slices on a serving platter or individual plates. Add the herbs to the bowl with the fennel and avocado and toss together. Add the cheese into the bowl and toss again, then mound the salad on top of the beetroot and serve.

potato salad

serves 4
- 700 g/1 lb 9 oz new potatoes
- 8 spring onions
- 250 ml/9 fl oz mayonnaise
- 1 tsp paprika
- salt and pepper
- 2 tbsp snipped fresh chives
  and a pinch of paprika,
  to garnish

1 Bring a large saucepan of lightly salted water to the boil. Add the potatoes and cook for 10–15 minutes, or until they are just tender.

2 Drain the potatoes and rinse them under cold running water until completely cold. Drain again. Transfer the potatoes to a bowl and reserve until required.

3 Using a sharp knife, slice the spring onions diagonally.

4 Mix the mayonnaise, paprika and salt and pepper to taste together in a bowl. Pour the mixture over the potatoes. Add the spring onions to the potatoes and toss together.

5 Transfer the potato salad to a serving bowl, and garnish with snipped chives and a pinch of paprika. Cover and leave to chill in the refrigerator until required.

wild rice salad

serves 4

- 225 g/8 oz wild rice
- 850 ml/1½ pints water
- 1 red pepper, skinned, deseeded and thinly sliced
- 1 yellow pepper, skinned, deseeded and thinly sliced
- 1 orange pepper, skinned, deseeded and thinly sliced
- ½ cucumber, quartered and sliced
- 1 orange, peeled, pith removed and sliced
- 3 ripe tomatoes, cut into chunks
- 1 red onion, finely sliced
- generous handful of chopped flat-leaf parsley

dressing

- 1 clove garlic, crushed
- 1 tbsp balsamic vinegar
- 2 tbsp extra virgin olive oil

1 Put the wild rice and water into a large pan and bring to the boil. Stir, cover and simmer for about 40 minutes or until the rice is tender but still firm to the bite. Uncover the rice for the last few minutes of cooking to allow any excess water to evaporate.

2 To make the dressing, put all the ingredients into a small screw-top jar and shake until well blended.

3 Drain the rice and turn into a large bowl. Pour over the dressing and mix in. Then mix in the sliced peppers, cucumber, orange, tomatoes, red onion and parsley and serve.

chilli-spiced paneer salad

serves 2

- 6 tbsp sunflower oil
- 225 g/8 oz paneer, cubed
- 1 tsp mustard seeds
- 1 tsp ground cumin
- 1 garlic clove, crushed
- 1 small green chilli pepper, deseeded and finely chopped
- 4 spring onions, finely chopped
- 85 g/3 oz baby salad leaves

tomato chutney

- 2 ripe tomatoes, skinned, deseeded and diced
- 1 shallot, finely chopped
- 2 tbsp sunflower oil
- 2 tsp lemon juice
- 1 tbsp chopped fresh coriander
- salt and pepper

1 To make the tomato chutney, place all the ingredients in a small bowl and mix together well. Chill in the refrigerator for 30 minutes.

2 Heat the oil in a large frying pan. Add the paneer cubes and fry over a medium–high heat for 4–5 minutes, turning frequently, until golden brown all over (take care as the oil may spit). Remove the paneer with a slotted spoon and drain on kitchen paper.

3 Carefully pour off half the hot oil from the pan. Add the mustard seeds and ground cumin to the remaining oil and fry for a few seconds. Stir in the garlic, chilli pepper and spring onions and fry for 1–2 minutes. Return the paneer to the pan and toss to coat well in the spicy mixture.

4 Divide the salad leaves between 2 serving plates. Top with the hot paneer. Spoon over the tomato chutney and serve immediately.

Index